
22 Aug

📍 Proms at Liverpool
☀ 1.00pm • Carwithen, Brahms
Dudok Quartet Amsterdam

Prom 47
7.30pm • Aretha Franklin: Queen of Soul
Sheléa, Jules Buckley Orchestra/Buckley

29 Aug

📍 Proms at Birmingham
☀ 1.00pm • Horowitz, Smyth, R. Clarke, Vaughan Williams, Wallen
Barnett-Jones, Lepper

Prom 57
7.30pm • Bach: Mass in B minor
soloists, Choir of the Age of Enlightenment, OAE/Butt

5 Sep

The Gaspard

23 Aug

Prom 48
7.30pm • Webern, Debussy/Dean, Brahms
Stagg, Australian World Orchestra/Mehta

30 Aug

Prom 58
8.00pm • Public Service Broadcasting
PSB, BBC SO/Buckley

6 Sep

Prom 67
7.30pm • Adès, Marsalis, Britten, Bernstein
Benedetti, RSNO/Søndergård

24 Aug

Prom 49
7.00pm • Birtwistle, Mahler
Alder, Connolly, CBSO Chorus, LSC, LSO/Rattle

Prom 50
☽ 10.15pm • Tavener, Tallis, MacMillan, Tye, Górecki, Sheppard, Byrd
The Sixteen/Christophers

31 Aug

Prom 59
7.30pm • Elgar: The Dream of Gerontius
soloists, Hallé Choir, London Philharmonic Choir, LPO/Gardner

7 Sep

Prom 68
AD **BSL** **R**
☀ 11.00am • Relaxed Prom: Marsalis, Britten, Bernstein | Benedetti, RSNO/Søndergård

Prom 69
7.00pm • Beethoven: Missa solemnis
soloists, Orchestre Révolutionnaire et Romantique/Gardiner

25 Aug

Prom 51
7.30pm • Lalo, Brahms, Franck
Lozakovich, BBC SO/Gabel

1 Sep

Prom 60
AD **BSL**
7.30pm • BBC Open Music Prom
BBC CO/Ryan

8 Sep

Prom 70
7.30pm • Barber, Coleman, Beethoven
Blue, Philadelphia Orchestra/Nézet-Séguin

26 Aug

Prom 52
7.30pm • Vaughan Williams, Debussy, Adès, Sibelius
Kuusisto, Finnish RSO/Collon

2 Sep

Prom 61
7.30pm • Walker, Beethoven
soloists, Chineke! Voices, Chineke! Orchestra/Edusei

9 Sep

Prom 71
7.30pm • Rachmaninov, Chausson, Saint-Saëns, Price
Batiashvili, Philadelphia Orchestra/Nézet-Séguin

27 Aug

Proms 53 & 54
AD **BSL** 2.00pm performance
☀ 2.00pm & 7.30pm • Earth Prom
BBC SSO/Palmer

3 Sep

Proms and the ENO at Printworks London
☀ 3.00pm & 8.00pm • Glass Handel | Costanzo, Condo, Singh, The ENO Orchestra/Kamensek, Bonas

Prom 62
7.00pm • Mahler
Berliner Philharmoniker/K. Petrenko

Prom 63
☽ 10.15pm • Neset
Neset et al., London Sinfonietta/Paterson

10 Sep

Prom 72
7.15pm • Wilson, Coleridge-Taylor/Parkin, Wagner, Mascagni, Verdi, Carwithen, Davydov/Parkin, Wood, Arne, Elgar/Dudley, Parry/Elgar, Trad.
Davidsen, Kanneh-Mason, BBC Singers, BBC SC & SO/Stasevska

28 Aug

Prom 55
☀ 11.30am • Organ Recital: Wagner/Westbrook/Laube, Franck, Alkan, Liszt/Laube | Laube

Prom 56
7.30pm • The South African Jazz Songbook
Mthembu, ESKA, Cross, Metropole Orkest/Wyatt

4 Sep

Prom 64
☀ 11.30am • Piano Recital: Beethoven
Schiff

Prom 65
7.30pm • Schnittke, Shostakovich
Zimmermann, Berliner Philharmoniker/K. Petrenko

At a Glance

For Season Listings, see pages 115–151 • For Contents, including details of feature articles, see pages 4–5

Vaughan Williams at 150

The Proms marks the 150th anniversary of Ralph Vaughan Williams, who led the revival of British music in the 20th century. Popular favourites such as the blissfully soaring *The Lark Ascending* and the haunting Tallis-inspired *Fantasia* take their place alongside the visceral Fourth Symphony and the rarely heard concertos for oboe and for tuba.

PROM 2 • 16 JULY
See also Proms 6, 10, 16, 32, 37, 39, 52 and Proms at Birmingham (29 August)

Proms Around the UK

This year sees the Monday-lunchtime Proms chamber-music series taking place across the UK – with venues in Belfast, Birmingham, Bristol, Cardiff, Glasgow, Liverpool and Truro. And, in a new partnership, Sage Gateshead plays host to a Prom exploring folk-music influences featuring its resident orchestra, the Royal Northern Sinfonia, under its new Principal Conductor, Dinis Sousa.

PROMS AT SAGE GATESHEAD
23 JULY

Virtual Aurality

Robert Ames – who led 2019's sci-fi music Prom – returns to conduct the first ever Gaming Prom. The Royal Philharmonic Orchestra is on hand to give an edge-of-the-seat, real-world rendering of soundtracks from titles including *Battlefield 2042* and *Kingdom Hearts*.

PROM 21 • 1 AUGUST

Keys of Life

Ten fingers, 88 keys – and limitless possibilities. Superstar Yuja Wang is among a dazzling array of pianistic talent appearing this summer, including Behzod Abduraimov, Alexander Gavrylyuk, Benjamin Grosvenor, Katia and Marielle Labèque, Francesco Piemontesi and Sir András Schiff.

PROM 35 • 12 AUGUST

To Aretha, with Respect

Marking the 80th anniversary of the remarkable 'Queen of Soul' and civil rights campaigner Aretha Franklin, American singer Sheléa (a star of the 2020 film *The Clark Sisters: First Ladies of Gospel*) joins Jules Buckley and the Jules Buckley Orchestra for a deep dive into an inspirational, gospel-charged catalogue.

PROM 47 • 22 AUGUST

Earth Stories

In the BBC's centenary year, the Earth Prom explores the work of the BBC's Natural History Unit, whose awe-inspiring films – with colourful soundtracks to match – have brought us closer to nature ever since Sir David Attenborough's *Zoo Quest* first hit our screens in 1954.

PROMS 53 & 54 • 27 AUGUST

Contents

Welcome to the 2022 BBC Proms

A very warm welcome to the BBC Proms of 2022, in the BBC's centenary year. When the BBC took over the running of the Proms in 1927 – just five years into its existence – it cemented a relationship between an organisation whose founding principles were to 'inform, educate and entertain' and a music festival that aspired to give greater access to the world's finest music. It was, and remains, a perfect partnership.

This year is also special for being the first full, eight-week Proms season since 2019. I am proud of the fact that we have found a way of presenting two adapted seasons, finding creative solutions to the restrictions created by the pandemic, and leading the way in the gradual renewal of orchestral life. This year is another step on that journey, with a return to works of a scale ideally suited to the Royal Albert Hall. Grand choral masterpieces such as Verdi's *Requiem* and Elgar's *The Dream of Gerontius* feature alongside symphonic works by Mahler, Bruckner and Shostakovich. We also welcome back the ambitious, multimedia family concerts that fill the Hall with young people, and it is a particular delight to be able to resume our series of Relaxed concerts, given as part of our continuing mission to welcome new audiences to the Proms.

At the centre of our BBC centenary celebrations are, of course, the family of BBC Orchestras and Choirs that form the core of the festival. They are also the driving force behind our programme of new commissions – one of the most distinctive features of their year-round programmes and central to the mission of the Proms. This year the range of contemporary work is wider than ever, including such individual voices as Academy Award-winning composer Hildur Guðnadóttir, performance artist Jennifer Walshe and innovative band Public Service Broadcasting, the last of which has been commissioned to create a work based around the BBC's own sound archive from the past 100 years. Reflecting the wider importance of broadcast orchestras, we also welcome three European radio orchestras as part of an international line-up that includes the Berliner Philharmoniker and Philadelphia Orchestra. And, while Radio 3 remains the cherished home of the Proms, we also benefit from partnerships with other parts of the BBC: this season sees a return of the CBeebies Prom and collaborations with the Natural History Unit and Radio 1 Relax.

As well as the BBC's big birthday, this year we celebrate several composer anniversaries, from César Franck and Ralph Vaughan Williams, born in 1822 and 1872 respectively, to those whose work may be less well known, such as Doreen Carwithen, Iannis Xenakis and George Walker, all of whom would have turned 100 this year. We also make a feature of the music of Ethel Smyth: the trailblazer who inspired a new generation of women composers, and whose masterpiece *The Wreckers* is one of three operas featured this summer. Exploring the less familiar has also allowed us to turn the spotlight onto instruments that rarely appear as soloists, with concertos showcasing the harp, theremin, tuba, percussion, viola, French horn and oboe.

In recent years we have presented a number of concerts away from the Royal Albert Hall, and this year 11 concerts will take place elsewhere, with eight across the UK including in Wales, Scotland and Northern Ireland. Our chamber series takes us to Battersea, Belfast, Birmingham, Bristol, Cardiff, Glasgow, Liverpool and Truro, while our Prom at Sage Gateshead draws on local community groups and marks the start of a longer-term relationship with the venue and its musical partners. We also pay our first visit to the magnificent Printworks in South-East London for a genre-defying performance of Philip Glass and Handel arias.

The partnership between the BBC and the Proms has taken Proms founder-conductor Henry Wood's vision of reaching the 'widest possible audience' to heights he could only dream of. A century since the BBC's first radio broadcast, today Radio 3 joins BBC Television, iPlayer, Sounds and the World Service in bringing our concerts to audiences around the globe. However you choose to join us this summer, we look forward to offering you the very best in classical music. I hope you will find much to enjoy.

David Pickard Director, BBC Proms

Welcome to the BBC Proms 2022. This year we are back with a bang. For the first time since 2019 we have a full, eight-week season with orchestras, soloists and ensembles from around the globe, as well as the world-class UK ensembles who formed the backbone of the 'Covid-adapted' Proms of 2020 and 2021. As always, the BBC Orchestras and Choirs are at the heart of this celebration of musical excellence. Every concert can be heard on Radio 3 and BBC Sounds, and 20 can be seen on TV and BBC iPlayer too. Last year marked an early and significant coming-together for audiences and performers alike, with uncertainty as to the continuing impact of the Covid-19 pandemic. This year we want audiences to feel intensely that the joy and communion of music-making is back. The Proms will bring you things you may already love and things you may not know about. Whichever is true, you can be sure to have a connection with those on stage. Discovery, connection, the unexpected – this is what Lord Reith was about when he established the BBC a century ago, and what Henry Wood was about when he co-founded the Proms. I invite you to dive in and immerse yourself in this true multiverse of music, wherever you are.

Alan Davey Controller, BBC Radio 3

Trapdoors

A short story by Barney Norris
Illustrations by Anna Wilson

She could still be with them through the music they had loved. She discovered this trapdoor quite by accident one Christmas afternoon, hiding in plain sight. She started experimenting with how widely it could be used over the next few weeks. The answer was that it worked for nearly anyone. Anyone who wasn't here any more, that was. Otherwise, there would have been no need to find a new way to be with them. She could have just called them up, and that would have been a truer way of speaking to them than listening to their music.

It started with her grandmother. Perhaps that was natural. The love Rachel had for her was the same pure feeling so many little girls carry with them all through the rest of their lives, once their grandmothers have passed away, the memory of happiness without the tellings-off or scolding that mothers or fathers are sometimes obliged to dish out, the memory of sweets slipped under the dining table, reading stories to one another, and every visit to Grandma's house having been special, every memory a red-letter day. By definition it could never be ordinary to be in the bedroom at Grandma's house, tucked up after lights out and looking up into the slope roof and its old black beams, imagining the mice that might walk along them at night and leave presents on her pillow if she got off to sleep quick enough, knowing the corn dollies on the dresser were watching over everything and would keep her safe, and make sure the mice left again before the morning just like the mice in *The Tailor of Gloucester*. It could never be ordinary because her grandparents' cottage wasn't home. It felt like one, the purest, most roast-chestnuts-and-carols feeling in the heart whenever she went there, but home was a half-hour drive away, with all her toys and schoolwork waiting for her to come back and finish it, with a flat roof above her bed that she'd decorated with glow-in-the-dark stars, and no mice, no corn dollies, no old beams. Visits to Grandma were escapes from the dailyness of things.

What they would do when they got to the cottage was go into the garden at first and play, and then there'd be lunch, which might be potatoes and cold meat, and then after lunch, if it rained or once Rachel and her brother Ed had tired themselves out, they'd throw themselves down onto the sofa in front of the TV and watch one of the videos. Grandma owned a tiny and precious collection of VHS tapes she'd recorded off the TV. Rachel and her brother would watch them on rotation whenever they visited, in the long lull of the afternoon when they didn't feel like running round any more, and the grown-ups were talking over tea in the front room or out on the patio if it was sunny, and they wanted something to fall asleep to before their grandfather came and made up the fire. Most of the time it was *The Pirates of Penzance*, which was the favourite, or *Les Misérables*, or sometimes they would watch *Swan Lake*. But another tape used to come out at Christmas: *The Nutcracker*, which Rachel and Ed never watched the rest of the year. Grandma would fish out the tape for them, brandish it as if it was treasure, feed it into the video player as if she were doing something rare and sacred, and Rachel remembered the whole of the rest of the world always falling away as the toymaker seemingly turned that girl into a tiny version of herself, like she was Alice in Wonderland, and showed her the world going on under her nose that she never noticed because it only came out at night. Just like *The Tailor of Gloucester* mice Rachel knew ran riot after dark in the beams. She watched the dances of *The Nutcracker* and believed every moment.

Just once, they went and saw the real thing. Grandma took her and Ed up to London, and they got off the train at Waterloo and caught a taxi over the river, London in winter laid out for them on either side, getting out of the taxi in Covent Garden to the din of voices, thousands of bodies pressing through that space to go and do their Christmas shopping. Grandma led them into the opera house through the little back door in the corner of Covent Garden, and all the time Rachel still didn't know where they were going. It was a secret, a Christmas surprise. She wasn't to find out until it started. Even when they stood in the Floral Hall, surrounded by all the other opera-goers,

she couldn't guess, because her mind just couldn't process it. This vast space, the glass walls, the light coming in, and all the champagne on its trays. Rachel remembered thinking it was a train station, perhaps they were going away to France, like the time they'd gone to Disneyland. But they went upstairs and round a curving corridor, then took a doorway into the auditorium, and Rachel was looking down on the stage of *The Nutcracker*. Somehow she knew as soon as she saw it.

> 66 It felt just like that visit to the opera house. A feeling too big for her to take in. She started to laugh. She supposed it was love. It felt like Grandma reaching out from the screen to hold her and say 'Remember we shared this. Remember our paths crossed.' 99

She took her grandmother's hand and squeezed, because she didn't know how to let out the feeling of what was happening to her. There they were together, up in the gods, Ed on Grandma's other side and probably holding her other hand, looking down on this thing that existed from TV as if they had stepped through the screen and right into it. Rachel found she had started to cry. Grandma became suddenly confused

and let go of Ed to crouch down and look at her.

'What's wrong, darling? Are there too many people for you?'

Rachel fought for breath. She looked for words.

'No,' she said. 'It's just very beautiful. I never imagined it.'

Now, of course, she could only imagine it. That was all she would be able to have again: the memory of holding her grandmother's hand, all the life that had burnt in that beautiful, kind woman only existing now in Rachel's imagination. It had been 10 years since Grandma died, and in the meantime there had been other losses, and the pain had got easier – she'd got used to it, she supposed. Loneliness built up like a coastal shelf, the layer on layer of goodbyes you didn't want to have to say, and in the end it all started to feel numb. Grandma was the first person she loved who she had to say goodbye to, and that had been awful, but 10 years later she had learnt not to say so. The more she talked to other people, the more she realised everyone felt this. Life, seen from one angle, was grief on grief, and it didn't do to say too much about your own because there was always someone else who was going through worse things. She let the loss of her grandmother settle on her, become part of her, ordinary as possible, like not being very good at long jump, or her first break-up, or jobs she'd interviewed for and hadn't got. Hide it in among everything else, and don't admit how much it mattered. Then it might not hurt as much.

And then she found herself decorating her first flat with her first live-in boyfriend, Matt, one unseasonably snowy early December. And on a Sunday afternoon when she'd done all her work and was ready for the week ahead, and Matt had been to the shops to buy things for a roast and got back quick because the shops weren't busy, so didn't need to start cooking for another hour, they had the idea of putting something on TV, but couldn't decide what they wanted to watch. Rachel scrolled through iPlayer while Matt climbed up on a chair to root through the back of the cupboard, trying to find the Quality Street he'd brought home from work, and she found herself hovering over a film of *The Nutcracker*. Not the same one she'd watched on VHS, she didn't think, but it was *The Nutcracker*, all the same. It was the ballet she used to watch at Christmas.

'Would you mind watching this?' she asked. 'We used to watch it when I was a kid.'

Matt glanced down from his perch on the chair at the words on the screen and smiled.

'Me too,' he said.

So Rachel pressed play on the film, and something extraordinary happened. It was like Grandma was in the room. At first she couldn't take in what she was feeling. Then she started to sob like a child. And, before Matt could even get down off the dining chair and cross the room to her, she realised it felt just like that visit to the opera house. A feeling

too big for her to take in. She started to laugh. She supposed it was love. It felt like Grandma reaching out from the screen to hold her and say, 'Remember we shared this. Remember our paths crossed.' Matt sat down by her.

'Are you OK?'

'Yeah,' she said.

66 She found Billie Holiday; she found Sting, whom her mum had fancied rotten; she found Everything but the Girl's *Amplified Heart* and Kate Bush and *Rumours*. Then she found a Fats Waller record he'd cut in 1922, and knew she had to buy it. 99

It was like a magic power the music had that changed the air and the light around her, turned the world into something different, something denser than it had been before the music started playing. She supposed it had lain dormant for so long because she just never listened to what her family had listened to. Grandma had never sat down with her on a Sunday afternoon, while the roast was cooking, to have a good old listen to Adele; those albums that formed the soundtrack to Rachel's life hadn't even been released back then. But, once Rachel started digging out what Grandma *had* loved, buying old records second-

hand of Gilbert and Sullivan, Mozart, Shirley Bassey, and putting them on the turntable Matt had brought with him when he moved in and lowering the needle and sitting back to listen, she found the same magic happened every time. For as long as the breath of a song or one side of a record, she could spend time with Grandma again.

The trick worked with her grandad too. With him things were a little more morbid because he'd loved Schubert's *Winterreise* and Strauss's *Four Last Songs*, which she bought and listened to till she was thoroughly depressed and couldn't stop staring at all the dead trees in their leaflessness whenever she set foot outside, compelled to imagine them as the souls of people, the stripped-back reality of people in winter when they dropped all pretence and showed their true faces. But Grandad had also liked Elgar, and she got on better with the 'Enigma' Variations, *The Dream of Gerontius*, the Cello Concerto. That all felt more like autumn music, so she listened to that more than she listened to Schubert to keep the winter feelings at bay. When she did put on Schubert now and then, she developed a liking for a song called 'An die Musik': 'To Music', she learnt after a quick internet search. It seemed very loving, almost like the end of a movie, and when she found a translation of the words online she discovered she loved them. They made her very happy. 'My love, in my grey hours, when I am caught in the whorl of living, you warm me out of myself.

Your voice escaping as a sigh, a quiet chord, opens the heaven of the past and lets us out.' She chopped and changed the words till they felt like her own. It was just how music felt to listen to, when she listened in memory of lost people.

And not just her grandparents. 'Swing low, sweet chariot' brought her close to a boy she'd loved at school, because it was sung at his funeral after he died in a car accident. 'Physical' by Olivia Newton-John made her smile and feel close to her aunt. She waited a long time before she tried the trick with her mother. Not because she didn't want it to work, but just because the grief was different. Her mother had died from pneumonia last year. They'd all gone to see her in the hospital on her last afternoon, thinking everything was fine, because they'd got her on a ventilator and everything seemed to be under control. Then they had gone back to the house where her mum and dad lived, thinking they'd return to the hospital and visit again the following morning, and got a call that told them different. Rachel still didn't know how to deal with what had happened. When she thought about it, it seemed like a dream. So she held off listening to her mother's music, because she was afraid that she couldn't bear it. Without quite interrogating what she was thinking, she let the thought settle like snow that she was grieving, and while that was happening she was a little weak, and she would need to wait until things were better before she could risk remembering her mother. Of course, she had it the wrong way round. It was remembering that would make her strong again. But she didn't see that for a long time. It only happened because one wet afternoon she found herself in the vinyl store in Wokingham, going through their stock, and finding that almost every record she pulled out seemed to remind her of her mother. It was very strange, like God speaking to her. She found Billie Holiday; she found Sting, whom her mum had fancied rotten; she found Everything but the Girl's *Amplified Heart* and Kate Bush and *Rumours*. Then she found a Fats Waller record he'd cut in 1922, and knew she had to buy it. That was the sound of her mother's kitchen on childhood afternoons: the joy of the stride piano, Fats Waller's huge hands covering half the keyboard – she'd read somewhere he had a 13-note reach – and the joy in his voice lighting up the smell of baking, or accompanying Mum's knitting, only paused for *The Archers*. Mum hadn't listened to Fats Waller on vinyl. For her generation CDs had been the future. But this had been her music on her happiest days, when she prepared meals for the week ahead and made jumpers and socks and hats for her children, singing along to 'Ain't Misbehavin''.

Rachel bought the record and took it home. Matt was working in the spare room, doing some marking. He stopped when he saw her pull up in her car, came out and opened the front door for her. He looked at her like he knew there was something the matter.

'Hey,' he said.

'Hello.' She kissed him as she passed him in the doorway.

'What have you got?' he asked her.

'Mum used to love listening to this,' she said.

Matt nodded, a little apprehensive. He never knew quite what to say when this came up. He'd been new on the scene when Rachel's mum died; they had never even met.

'Let's play it.'

Rachel went through to the living room while Matt switched on the kettle. She took the record out of its sleeve, put it on the turntable, turned it on, lowered the needle. She looked out of the window at the street as Fats Waller started playing. He had struck these notes a hundred years ago, a continent away, on the other side of an ocean that took weeks to cross back then, in a world that must have seemed so different, though he must have felt life was the same puzzle Rachel did, to sing these songs, to make her feel like this now. The feeling cut through across those 100 years, the commonality of people, the shared heart beating. She thought of him sitting in a studio somewhere, or maybe in a concert hall, beating out a rhythm. And she thought of her mother, 75 years later, getting on with her knitting as the light faded out of the day.

Across the road from her flat, the family who had moved into the house opposite were locking the front door to go for their afternoon walk. A man and a woman and a baby in a pram. Life happening and happening, waves that never ended. One day this place would be that child's distant past. One day those parents would only live in memories. And perhaps the child in that pram today would discover that, when she listened to the right music, it would seem as if her parents were in the room with her.

Matt brought a cup of tea over to her. She took it in her hands, kept looking out the window. He put his arms around her and they watched together as the young family headed off towards the park. Rachel felt like her mum was also standing with her. She wished she could introduce her to Matt. She wished she could say, 'Look! Look at the life I'm building.' This was as close as she would ever get. Mum had come through the trapdoor of the music into the room, and Rachel almost felt like she was home as Fats Waller started to play 'Don't Get Around Much Any More'. She thought of 'An die Musik'.

My love, in my grey hours, when I am caught in the whorl of living, you warm me out of myself. Your voice escaping as a sigh, a quiet chord, opens the heaven of the past and lets us out. ●

Barney Norris is a playwright and novelist. This year he will direct his new play *We Started To Sing* at the Arcola Theatre in London; publish his fourth novel, *Undercurrent* (Doubleday); and create a new play called *The Invisible Man* with Derren Brown.

Anna Wilson is an Australian illustrator who has spent much of her adult life travelling the world. Her work is inspired by her love of places, people, weather, beautiful shapes, lines and light. She currently lives in Edinburgh.

Aretha, *Queen of Soul*

Ahead of a Prom celebrating 80 years since Aretha Franklin's birth, **KEVIN LE GENDRE** reflects on the singer's unique musicality, as well as her role as the voice of Black America

In the history of Black music a title or moniker is not bestowed lightly upon an artist. Not only does the accolade have to be earned, it has to be continually justified through performance in real time, on stage – that unforgiving setting in which all challengers have to, as the African American vernacular holds, show and prove. Aretha Franklin, who died four years ago this summer, became the 'Queen of Soul' because, whenever she stood in front of an audience and sang, she revealed the unimaginable, breathtaking beauty of her voice as well as its fathomless emotional depths. People were simultaneously enchanted and uplifted.

Nowhere is this more apparent than the iconic concert she gave at the New Temple Missionary Baptist Church in Los Angeles in January 1972, later released as the best-selling live album *Amazing Grace*. She appeared with a stellar band that included the masterful guitarist Cornell Dupree and the Southern California Community Choir, whose smouldering harmonies brilliantly enhanced her lead. But it was Franklin who really lit the fire, negotiating a broad repertoire that showed how she was able to cross several stylistic borders all the while bringing her vocal ingenuity to the fore. She did nothing less than make every song her own, regardless of its provenance. The high point of the concert saw her glide seamlessly

◀ The 'Queen of Soul' Aretha Franklin pictured onstage in 1970, two years before she recorded the live album *Amazing Grace*

from Thomas A. Dorsey's gospel standard 'Precious Lord, Take My Hand' to Carole King's pop anthem 'You've Got a Friend'. It was an electrifying moment. Arguably, Franklin secured her place in the canon of modern music (of any description) in the six minutes that elapsed during the imaginative marriage of those two songs, moving as she did with such self-possession, passion and attention to detail. She soared and swirled in the upper register and carefully fluttered in the lower; and, if she stretched notes for melismatic effect, she kept absolute focus on pitch and time. Between the first and the second theme her delivery pivoted from ecstasy to melancholy, but she did not lose her grip on the overarching narrative of solidarity.

The *Amazing Grace* album means a lot to American singer-songwriter Sheléa, who performs Franklin's repertoire with the Jules Buckley Orchestra on 22 August. 'I have fond memories as my mom played it when we were on our way to church,' she says. 'Her conviction touched me deeply – even as a young girl.' That priceless ability to engage listeners and make them believe in the story being told can be ascribed to a number of things in Franklin's life. The fact that she was raised in the Black church in Detroit, the daughter of Reverend C. L. Franklin, and was well versed in the art of singing gospel was pivotal, but so too was her musicianship. Aretha was a highly accomplished pianist who had debuted as a jazz artist, recording fine renditions of standards such as

'Skylark' and 'But Beautiful' in the early 1960s before switching to R&B a few years later and helping, along with the likes of Sam Cooke and Ray Charles, to redefine the genre as soul. Thereafter she embarked upon an incredible run of hits that included 'I Never Loved a Man the Way I Love You', 'Chain of Fools', 'Do Right Woman, Do Right Man', '(You Make Me Feel Like) A Natural Woman', 'I Say a Little Prayer' and 'Spanish Harlem'. Each tune has enormous meaning for countless listeners, Black and White, around the world – those in need of solace by way of melody and elation, or in the form of rhythm, as is the case on the irresistibly funky 'Rocksteady'. Franklin performed all these pieces as an extension of her life experience, as if every beat was her heartbeat.

66 The soul and conviction just oozed out of her. It was in her DNA. When she opened her mouth to sing, you believed her every time. And, although she had incredible technique, she didn't completely rely on vocal acrobatics to prove she was a good singer. She simply knew she was. 99

'What made Aretha so special as a vocalist was her ability to bring soul and emotion to every song so effortlessly,'

Aretha Franklin pictured alongisde Martin Luther King Jr; as a teenager she toured with the civil rights leader and, following his assassination in 1968, she sang at his funeral

'Let music swell the breeze': Franklin performing 'America' ('My country, 'tis of thee') at Barack Obama's presidential inauguration ceremony in January 2009

says Sheléa. 'There was nothing contrived in her performances. The soul and conviction just oozed out of her. It was in her DNA. When she opened her mouth to sing, you believed her every time. And, although she had incredible technique, she didn't completely rely on vocal acrobatics to prove she was a good singer. She simply knew she was.' Like Franklin, Sheléa learnt to play the piano at a young age, and she appreciates the performances in which Franklin accompanied herself: 'I can sense she felt most at home while singing at the piano.' But her favourite performance is from the 1998 Grammy Awards, when Franklin sang Puccini's 'Nessun dorma', filling in for an ailing Luciano Pavarotti: 'It was a masterclass. She didn't shy away from being Aretha even while singing an opera aria.'

Bear in mind that the classical world was largely out of bounds for Black women of Franklin's generation, as the experience of her illustrious peer Nina Simone showed (Simone was denied entry to study piano at Philadelphia's Curtis Institute). The empowerment Franklin gave to others in crossing these stylistic lines was consolidated by her extensive activism during the American Civil Rights Movement. Indeed, her anthems 'Think' and 'Respect' were uncompromising demands for racial and gender equality. Franklin was encouraged to take part in the movement by her father. She toured with colossal figures such as Martin Luther King Jr and Harry Belafonte, in addition to performing free concerts in order to shine a light on the daily struggles of African Americans. 'She used her platform to challenge people to vote and, in her words, "stand up for decency",' notes Sheléa. 'Aretha wasn't just an entertainer. She was a socially conscious artist who didn't just shut up and sing.'

Indeed, she became the grand musical matriarch who would continue to inspire and collaborate with several new generations of artists, from Luther Vandross and Marcus Miller in the 1980s, to Lauryn Hill in the 1990s and Ron 'Amen-Ra' Lawrence in the 2000s. The fact that Franklin had major hits during these decades ('Jump to It', 'Get It Right' and 'A Rose Is Still a Rose') emphasised her relevance to the ever-evolving canon of Black pop. And, as America changed politically, it was entirely fitting that Franklin was the woman to underscore its turning points. It is hard to imagine anybody else singing with the gravitas she exuded at President Obama's inauguration in 2009, which, lest we forget, was a landmark event – the arrival of a Black president of whom Franklin dared to dream in her formative years. Her many freedom songs, with their artful blend of secular and sacred traditions, gave balm to those who believed that a better world was always possible. The Soul Nation needed a queen, and it found one in Aretha Franklin. ●

Kevin Le Gendre writes about music and literature for publications including *Echoes* and *Jazzwise*, and is the author of *Don't Stop the Carnival: Black British Music* (2018) and *Hear My Train A Comin': The Songs of Jimi Hendrix* (2020). He is a presenter of BBC Radio 3's *J to Z*.

Aretha Franklin: Queen of Soul
PROM 47 • 22 AUGUST

KENNEDY STREET BY ARRANGEMENT WITH UNITED TALENT AGENCY PRESENTS

GEORGE BENSON 2022

JUNE 17	**BOURNEMOUTH** INTERNATIONAL CENTRE
JUNE 19	**CARDIFF** ST DAVID'S HALL
JUNE 20	**MANCHESTER** BRIDGEWATER HALL
JUNE 22	**LEEDS** FIRST DIRECT ARENA
JUNE 24	**GLASGOW** ROYAL CONCERT HALL
JUNE 26	**LONDON** ROYAL ALBERT HALL
JUNE 28	**BIRMINGHAM** SYMPHONY HALL
JUNE 29	**SOUTHEND** CLIFFS PAVILION

TICKETLINE.CO.UK • TICKETMASTER.CO.UK

KENNEDY STREET AND LIVE NATION PRESENTS

GLADYS KNIGHT

THE WAY WE WERE · BEST THING THAT EVER HAPPENED TO ME
BABY DON'T CHANGE YOUR MIND · MIDNIGHT TRAIN TO GEORGIA
LICENCE TO KILL · HELP ME MAKE IT THROUGH THE NIGHT

JUNE 2022

18	**MANCHESTER** O2 APOLLO
19	**BIRMINGHAM** SYMPHONY HALL
21	**BOURNEMOUTH** INTERNATIONAL CENTRE
22	**LIVERPOOL** M&S BANK ARENA
23	**NOTTINGHAM** ROYAL CONCERT HALL
25	**CARDIFF** MOTORPOINT ARENA
26	**LEEDS** FIRST DIRECT ARENA
27	**GLASGOW** ROYAL CONCERT HALL
29	**LONDON** ROYAL ALBERT HALL
30	**LONDON** ROYAL ALBERT HALL

With special guest
MARK KINGSWOOD

TICKETLINE.CO.UK   TICKETMASTER.CO.UK   OR THE VENUES DIRECT
GLADYSKNIGHT.COM

GK

FROM THE USA ★ BACK BY DEMAND ★ BACK TO BACK HITS

2022 THE TEMPTATIONS & THE FOUR TOPS

BALL OF CONFUSION ★ GET READY   REACH OUT I'LL BE THERE ★ WALK AWAY RENEE
CLOUD NINE ★ TREAT HER LIKE A LADY   LOCO IN ACAPULCO ★ SUGAR PIE HONEY
MY GIRL ★ PAPA WAS A ROLLIN' STONE   STANDING IN THE SHADOWS OF LOVE ★ BERNADETTE

PLUS SPECIAL GUESTS **ODYSSEY**   USE IT UP AND WEAR IT OUT ★ INSIDE OUT   *ODYSSEY NOT APPEARING AT*
GOING BACK TO MY ROOTS ★ NATIVE NEW YORKER   *SOUTHEND CLIFFS PAVILION*

30 SEP	**MANCHESTER AO ARENA**	AO-ARENA.COM
01 OCT	**LEEDS FIRST DIRECT ARENA**	FIRSTDIRECTARENA.COM
02 OCT	**LIVERPOOL M&S BANK ARENA**	MANDSBANKARENA.COM
05 OCT	**SOUTHEND CLIFFS PAVILION***	THECLIFFSPAVILION.CO.UK
06 OCT	**NOTTINGHAM MOTORPOINT ARENA**	MOTORPOINTARENANOTTINGHAM.COM
07 OCT	**BOURNEMOUTH INTERNATIONAL CENTRE**	BHLIVETICKETS.CO.UK
09 OCT	**BIRMINGHAM UTILITA ARENA**	UTILITAARENABHAM.CO.UK
10 OCT	**CARDIFF MOTORPOINT ARENA**	MOTORPOINTARENACARDIFF.CO.UK
11 OCT	**LONDON THE O2**	THEO2.CO.UK

WWW.TICKETLINE.CO.UK WWW.TICKETMASTER.CO.UK

A KENNEDY STREET ENTERPRISES & LIVE NATION PRESENTATION

FRANKIE VALLI

AND THE **FOUR SEASONS**
GREATEST HITS
UK TOUR 2022

"DECEMBER, 1963 (OH, WHAT A NIGHT)"
"SHERRY" • "WALK LIKE A MAN"
"CAN'T TAKE MY EYES OFF YOU"
"BIG GIRLS DON'T CRY" • "RAG DOLL"
"WHO LOVES YOU" • "GREASE"
"WORKING MY WAY BACK TO YOU"
"MY EYES ADORED YOU"

JUNE 26TH	**BIRMINGHAM RESORTS WORLD ARENA**
JUNE 28TH	**LIVERPOOL M&S BANK ARENA**
JUNE 29TH	**NOTTINGHAM MOTORPOINT ARENA**

JULY 1ST & 2ND   LONDON ROYAL ALBERT HALL
WITH THE ROYAL PHILHARMONIC CONCERT ORCHESTRA

PRESENTED BY **KENNEDY STREET** AAA **LIVE NATION** WWW.FRANKIEVALLIFOURSEASONS.COM

New
Glass/

Minimalism meets Baroque in Anthony Roth
Costanzo's bold multifaceted project drawing
together a plethora of top-flight creatives.
He talks to GEORGE HALL about mixing Glass
with Handel, and finding new audiences

/Handel
with Care

Trailblazing American counter-tenor Anthony Roth Costanzo has a keen eye for multi-arts projects but his latest is uniquely far-reaching. *Glass Handel* contrasts vocal solos by Handel and Philip Glass, but also weaves in dance, live painting, music videos and audio soundscapes. Its Proms performance take place in South London's industrial events space, Printworks, following its premiere performances in 2018 in Philadelphia and New York.

When I speak to Costanzo, he's at home in New York preparing for productions at the Metropolitan Opera – aptly, Philip Glass's *Akhnaten* and Handel's *Rodelinda* – followed by a period with the New York Philharmonic as Artist-in-Residence. The idea of putting together Glass and Handel came when he was programming his first album, he explains. 'The label wanted something really personal. I thought long and hard and realised that, as a singer, Handel really defined me – I had cut my teeth on Handel, made my Met debut with it and I'd sung it all over the world. But then, when I sang *Akhnaten* at English National Opera in 2016, it changed how I thought about things.'

Costanzo's first time singing *Akhnaten* proved difficult in terms of endurance: 'It only became possible when I started to think about what I had to do technically

◀ Frock tactics: Anthony Roth Costanzo in *Glass Handel* (Philadelphia, 2018), wearing one of three costumes by Raf Simons

to sing Handel, and then applied that to Glass. Similarly, while performing the Glass – which is heavily based on repeating patterns – I had to find ways to keep it alive, even if the music didn't provide change in certain ways. That turned out to be a helpful approach to bring to Handel. So I started to think about placing the two of them together, and found all kinds of affinities.'

He went on to create *Glass Handel*, 'which is about how the music can be seen through the eyes of different artists who are stars in their own art forms. Part of the reason for this was that I was thinking about "gateway" audiences, so to speak, for classical music – people already interested in the arts, be it painting or dance or film or fashion.'

Costanzo's distinguished collaborators include painter George Condo, sound artist Jason Singh, choreographer Justin Peck and Co-Creative Director of Prada, Raf Simons. Joining co-producers and creators Cecilia Dean and Cath Brittan, they formed the team behind the development of the project.

'I wanted to create something non-static involving all these different elements. We came up with this idea of producing one music video for each track on the album – little art films that could engage people digitally.'

In fact, a new version is being created for the Proms performance in a co-production with English National Opera, which promises to be unlike anything previously performed in

the UK. Costanzo is particularly happy that his *Akhnaten* conductor, Karen Kamensek, will be involved.

'We are really reinventing it for the Proms, making it an experience that will be tailored to the city, the space that we have chosen and the time that we live in. We also feel very lucky that Philip Glass is giving us a world premiere. We will have a new video that goes along with that. We've learnt from the previous versions and I'm hopeful that this will be our best.'

Costanzo is delighted that *Glass Handel* will take place at Printworks because the show doesn't fit into a typical seated auditorium. 'Printworks is essentially a nightclub, and I love the idea that young people have an association with it.'

'What happened to a certain extent in New York and Philadelphia – and I hope this continues in London – is that we got some people who have never really engaged with classical music, or have no particular vision of what it is, who will walk into Printworks and see an incredible dancer, or a painting being made. Maybe they've come because they are interested in George Condo, or some other aspect of it, and they'll find themselves thinking, "You know, this music is actually quite beautiful."' ●

George Hall writes widely on classical music and opera for publications including *The Stage*, *Opera*, *Opera News*, *Opera Now* and *BBC Music Magazine*. He co-edited *The Proms in Pictures* (BBC Books, 1995) with Matías Tarnopolsky.

Glass Handel

PROMS AND ENO AT PRINTWORKS LONDON
3 SEPTEMBER, 3.00pm & 8.00pm

Rolling with **the Punches**

How do the circumstances of a work's premiere define its future
success? IVAN HEWETT reveals the inauspicious beginnings of
several key pieces featured this season

Every piece of music has its own life story, which, as with every kind of life story, begins with a birth. The first performance of a new piece is politely clapped; the music fulfils its role of gilding an occasion – celebrating a prince's birthday or a town's centenary. But, in many cases, that is it: the piece vanishes quietly from history. Most likely the score itself disappears, unless some antiquarian tucks it away in a library, ready to be discovered centuries later.

In a small number of cases the first chapter is not also the last. The piece survives beyond its birth. It lives for a second day, or a year, or perhaps even centuries, as other performers carry the piece to new places, new venues and later eras. In the case of a very lucky few, they enter that charmed circle of pieces that seem destined for immortality. These pieces are the exemplars of the tradition and touchstones of excellence. As such, Beethoven's and Brahms's symphonies, Bach's Brandenburg Concertos and Stravinsky's ballets seem now to be beyond the reach of misfortune. They've survived plagues, world wars and financial crashes; and, assuming civilisation itself survives climate change and ideological convulsion, it's a fair bet that these pieces will survive as well.

Given that these survivals are so rare, it's tempting to look back at their birth to see whether the signs were propitious and the stars and planets in alignment. We imagine that such important pieces must come into the world 'trailing clouds of glory', their stature blazingly evident in their origins, like saints who emerge from the womb already able to pray in Latin or cure illness.

> 66 The connection between a work's premiere and its subsequent fate is far from predictable. The history of music is littered with pieces whose premieres could be described as 'auspicious', *ie* were wildly successful and praised on all sides, but which have since vanished. 99

Of course, it's not like that. The first performance of any masterpiece wasn't announced as such; it was just one in a series of events happening in that month in that venue. Like any concert, it was liable to be spoilt by all kinds of banal accidents. In earlier times, when life was less micromanaged and accidents more frequent, events we like to imagine as surefire successes were beset with difficulties that threatened to obscure the music entirely. Take the famous all-Beethoven 'monster concert' of December 1808 in Vienna, when the composer directed premieres of his latest works, including the Fifth Symphony. Everything was against it: the freezing cold weather coupled with the lack of heating in the Theater an der Wien, the clash with a rival concert at a nearby theatre, the mediocre orchestra.

Of the many factors that could jeopardise the survival of a new work, a poor performance is undoubtedly the commonest. It's painful to think how many great works have been revealed to the world in a distorted or even mangled state. In the case of Elgar's *The Dream of Gerontius* the problem seems to have been especially acute. One eyewitness at the premiere on 3 October 1900 lamented that 'the chorus did not know the parts they were trying to sing ... there were times when they seemed to be a whole semitone out and when the orchestra, disregarding the directions on the score, would play *fortissimo* in order to drag them back to the true pitch. The whole thing was a nightmare.' In the case of works written in a modernist atonal style it's fair to say that, until Pierre Boulez and a few others raised standards in the 1960s and 1970s, performances must have been almost universally bad. Schoenberg's quip 'My music is not modern, it is just badly played' had more than a grain of truth.

These are the purely negative factors that weigh down or even destroy a premiere. Alongside them are those factors that, although apparently banal and negative at the time, can – if the piece survives and is elevated to the canon of 'great works' – take on a positive aspect. Myth-making is a powerful force that can gild banal

◀ A cartoon in the German newspaper *Die Zeit* depicting the 1913 'Skandalkonzert', at which several members of the audience came to blows

> 66 The choir, audibly dragged down by a single tenor in the first chorus, had flattened by degrees until in the last number of the first part there was half a tone between them and the orchestra. I can guarantee the truth of this as I, being the bass soloist and having to sing a part above the chorus, had to choose between them and was not happy with either.

Harry Plunket Greene, the Irish baritone who sang the Priest's solo 'Go forth upon thy journey, Christian soul' at the 1900 premiere of Elgar's *The Dream of Gerontius*, recalls the unfortunate performance

accidents with meaning; even the lack of heating at Beethoven's 'monster concert' can seem meaningful, a tragicomic symbol of the great composer's endless struggles against the world.

In any case some accidents, far from being banal, seem almost to have been conjured by fate to lend grandeur to a premiere. Take the first performance of Prokofiev's Fifth Symphony on 13 January 1945, conducted by the composer himself in the Great Hall of the Moscow Conservatory. Coming towards the end of what came to be known as the Great Patriotic War, when the remnants of the defeated German army had at last been driven from Russian soil, this was bound to be a hugely emotional event. Just before the performance began, news was received of a significant victory against the German army on the Vistula in Poland, an event that had to be marked by an artillery salute. The pianist Sviatoslav Richter described what happened next: 'When Prokofiev mounted the podium and silence set in, artillery salvos suddenly thundered. His baton was already raised. He waited, and until the cannon fire ceased he didn't begin. There was something very significant, very symbolic in this. It was as if all of us – including Prokofiev – had reached some kind of shared turning point.'

At the opposite pole to mighty affirmations such as this are those poignant or sinister absences, *ie* works whose first performance never actually took place owing to political pressures. There were numerous 'non-premieres'

during the 70-year history of the Soviet Union, though perhaps the best-known of them was Shostakovich's Fourth Symphony. Days before the scheduled premiere in December 1936 the journal *Soviet Art* announced that the composer had withdrawn the piece, on the grounds that it suffered from 'grandiosomania' and 'no longer represented the composer's current artistic convictions'. A more likely explanation was that the composer was anxious about the work's ear-scraping dissonance, which he knew would not be well received. Some months previously his opera *The Lady Macbeth of the Mtsensk District* had been denounced in the government-controlled newspaper *Pravda* under the headline 'Muddle Instead of Music'.

To avoid the fate of many of his friends and allies, who had vanished to the Gulag or been murdered, Shostakovich had to make a very public show of penitence. He provided it with his Symphony No. 5, which struck a deliberately sober and serious note. 'A Soviet artist's practical creative reply to just criticism' was how the composer reportedly described it, but more evident to listeners at the 1937 premiere was its tragic undertones, prompted surely by the horrors of Stalin's Great Terror, which was then at its height.

Shostakovich's Fourth Symphony had to wait until 1961 for its premiere, which turned out to be a triumph. In that case the long delay before acceptance had nothing to do with the music itself; there were no negative first impressions to overcome. The slow acceptance of Elgar's *Gerontius* is different, because first impressions at the premiere in 1903 were indeed mostly negative, though for reasons that were only partly to do with the wretched performance. The piece also suffered from lingering anti-papist sentiment in Britain, thanks to its deeply Catholic vision of the afterlife (Charles Villiers Stanford sneered that it 'stank of incense'). But there was no scandal; the almost exclusively Protestant audience was polite. It was only with the arrival of difficult and often abrasively dissonant modernism that audiences would forgo politeness and start shouting their disapproval.

The first performance of Stravinsky's *Rite of Spring* is the go-to example of the scandalous modern premiere, but two months before, in March 1913, a concert of orchestral music and song from the three most notorious modernists in Vienna caused a similar if not greater commotion. Here the sound of face-slapping and challenges to duels threatened to drown the sound of the music. One of the offending items was the *Six Pieces for Orchestra* by Anton Webern, a normally mild-mannered man who on this occasion lost his temper. A Viennese newspaper reported that 'Herr von Webern shouted from his box that the "whole pack" should be thrown out, which prompted a response that the entire body of musicians should be sent to the lunatic asylum. The raging and screaming could not be stopped. It was not at all unusual to see gentlemen in the audience climb, in breathless haste and ape-like agility, over several rows to box the ears of the objects of their fury.'

When the Dust Settles

Scottish composer Anna Meredith reflects on the premiere of her piece *Five Telegrams*

I've been lucky enough to have a number of my pieces premiered at the BBC Proms over the years and, looking back, they've been real markers in my development and evolution as a composer. My biggest and most recent was *Five Telegrams*, which I wrote for the First Night of the Proms and the opening of the Edinburgh International Festival in 2018.

The piece was a collaboration with visual art and projection-mapping company 59 Productions, and incorporated visuals that were projected onto the inside and outside of the Royal Albert Hall. The music at the premiere was performed by the BBC Symphony Orchestra, BBC Proms Youth Ensemble and National Youth Choir of Great Britain both to an audience inside the Hall and an audience outside standing in Hyde Park. It was a massive undertaking, and – in addition to the actual writing – I remember much of the preceding two years being filled with planning, researching, testing, meetings, technical adjustments, rethinking and the frequent feeling of being daunted and overwhelmed.

After so much preparation the premiere of a piece can sometimes feel a little anticlimactic. You anxiously follow the score in your head or worry about things that might go wrong. It's hard to be 'in the moment' and often impossible to experience the piece as if listening for the first time. With *Five Telegrams*, however, it actually *was* the first time the piece had been fully performed! In the run-up the projections could only be prepped by night and the BBC Symphony Orchestra could only rehearse by day – so the two only came together at the premiere.

Finally seeing and hearing the piece on such an enormous scale after so much small-scale plotting and score-peering was amazing. The size and volume and love and work we'd all poured into it gave the performance – for me at least – the direct and visceral impact that is so much part of what I'm looking for in my writing.

It was obviously reassuring on the night to get the thoughts of people whose ears I trust – who perhaps knew what I was hoping to do with the piece. But it was also lovely to receive messages from strangers in the audience – people who had come to the piece with no expectations, experiencing it in the way we had intended: stood outside, listening and watching.

After my first Proms commission, *froms*, which was written for the 2008 Last Night, I received everything from hate mail to marriage proposals, and now that my writing straddles so many different areas I'm used to hearing a range of opinions. So I try to wait until the dust has settled on a piece before I evaluate it on my own terms – to see what worked and what didn't. Though it's not always the case, with hindsight I can say I am hugely proud of *Five Telegrams*. I think it's the strongest and best orchestral music I've written.

Ekaterina Berezina dances the part of the Girl in Bartók's *The Miraculous Mandarin* (Moscow Classical Ballet, 2016), whose 'indecency' so scandalised audiences at the Cologne premiere that it was banned by the city's mayor

When an ear-bendingly aggressive and dissonant musical idiom is placed at the service of a violent scenario, a scandal is even more likely – as in the case of Bartók's 'pantomime' *The Miraculous Mandarin*, in which a prostitute and her accomplices beat and rob passing men. The premiere in 1926 in Cologne outraged the audience, and the city mayor Konrad Adenauer (who after the war became the first Chancellor of the new Federal Republic of Germany) actually banned any further performances.

But were these scandals such a disaster? There's nothing like a whiff of notoriety to whip up interest in a piece. Once it is in circulation and becomes familiar, audiences can begin to hear it in a different way. The vast scale and difficulty of Beethoven's Symphony No. 9, which puzzled even sympathetic critics at its premiere, in Vienna in 1824, eventually seemed acceptable – even sublime – as the Romantic aesthetic already dominant in literature and the visual arts finally penetrated the musical world.

What all this tells us is that the connection between a work's premiere and its subsequent fate is far from predictable. The history of music is littered with pieces whose premieres could be described as 'auspicious', *ie* were wildly successful and praised on all sides, but which have since vanished. Those that actually survived to enter the repertoire needed other things on their side: musical quality, committed performers to champion them, connections to world-shaping historical events. Being notorious helps, certainly, as does its opposite: being perfectly in tune with the values or prejudices of the audience. But, even with all these advantages, a piece can simply fade away.

Still, a good premiere certainly gives a piece a better chance of survival. Compared to the hazards that attended premieres of works in the past, a Proms premiere seems as safe as houses *(see 'Mood Music', pages 72–77)*. A technically proficient, polished performance is practically guaranteed, and the nationwide broadcast on Radio 3, plus the many more listeners worldwide, ensures the piece has the best start in life. The other essential thing a new piece needs is your undivided attention. So be sure to give it. You never know, you may be witnessing the birth of a classic. ●

Ivan Hewett is a critic and broadcaster who for nine years presented BBC Radio 3's *Music Matters*. He writes for *The Telegraph*, teaches at the Royal College of Music and is the author of an examination of modern music, *Healing the Rift* (Bloomsbury, 2003).

BLACK MASTERPIECE
LIMITED EDITION

In honour of the 20th anniversary of the
Steinway Crown Jewels series we present
BLACK MASTERPIECE – an edition
limited to 20 models worldwide
with a sophisticated black look
that will delight lovers of
clear design.

BLACK MASTERPIECE grand pianos are issued as model B 211cm and are equipped
with **SPIRIO** | *r*, the most modern technology Steinway currently has to offer.

Steinway Hall London W1U 2DB For more information or to arrange a private appointment at our
London showrooms, please call: **0207 487 3391** info@steinway.co.uk

STEINWAY & SONS

Hear every note, feel every beat

Since 1972, we've created unforgettable sound experiences with technical expertise and award-winning British design, crafting speakers that will make your hair stand on end and take your breath away.

Learn more at **monitoraudio.com**

ROYAL PHILHARMONIC ORCHESTRA

2022–23 Season

Featuring
Vasily Petrenko
Sir Andrew Davis
Isata Kanneh-Mason
Jennifer Pike
Alexander Shelley
Arabella Steinbacher
Anu Tali
and more

With music by composers including **Mahler, Shostakovich, Wagner, Beethoven, Tchaikovsky, Fauré, Clara Schumann, Vaughan Williams, Dvořák** and **Grieg**

RPO 75th Anniversary Gala Concert with Music Director Vasily Petrenko, Credit: Ben Wright, September 2021

Join the journey | Discover more at **rpo.co.uk**

ARTS COUNCIL ENGLAND

Supported using public funding by ARTS COUNCIL ENGLAND

RHS
HAMPTON
COURT PALACE
GARDEN FESTIVAL

4–9 July 2022
RHS Members' Days 4 & 5 July

Gardens, plants & flowers | Unique shopping | Expert advice & demos
Grow your own | Live music | Food markets | Family fun

Book now at rhs.org.uk

RHS Registered Charity no. 222879 / SC038262

How to Get to
Carnegie Hall

Performance coach and psychologist **NOA KAGEYAMA** shares
some tips and strategies – including some borrowed from
sports research – that musicians can adopt to ensure that
practice makes perfect

We've all heard the joke about the tourist in New York City who approaches a musician on 57th Street and asks, 'How do you get to Carnegie Hall?' – to which the musician replies 'Practice, practice, practice.'

It's no surprise to hear that it takes decades of hard work and dedication to attain the high level of skill and musicianship on display at the great concert halls around the world, but what does 'Practice, practice, practice' actually mean? If we could be a fly on the wall of our favourite musicians' practice rooms, what exactly would we see?

If you took music lessons yourself as a child, you might associate the word 'practice' with 'repetition'. At least, I certainly did. From the time I had my first violin lesson at the age of 2, through my conservatory years, and even into graduate school, I operated under the assumption that the more time I put in, and the more 'perfect' repetitions I could squeeze into any given practice session, the better I would ultimately play.

After all, when young musicians begin their musical journey, practice is often assigned in units of time or numbers of repetition: 'Practise 30 minutes per day' or 'Start every day's practice with five minutes of scales and arpeggios', for instance; or even 'Practise picking up your

bow with rounded fingers and thumb 100 times before your next lesson' or 'Play through the first movement of your concerto twice a day without stopping'.

There's nothing inherently wrong with repetition, of course, but when repetition itself is framed as the goal, there can be a tendency for practice to morph into mindless finger gymnastics.

This is where a young musician might start at the beginning of a piece and play until they hear something that doesn't sound quite right. At which point they may stop, go back a few bars, and play the passage again. And again. And again. And perhaps a few more times, until their fingers intuitively autocorrect and produce something closer to the ideal that they hear in their head.

Walk through any conservatory or music school in the world, and you'll hear this pattern being repeated over and over. And, while this approach to practising does work to a degree, it has its limits.

The best practisers appear to approach practising differently. Instead of engaging in mindless repetition, their practice is more intentional.

Hungarian violinist Leopold Auer – whose students included Jascha Heifetz, Nathan Milstein and countless others – once said, 'Practise with your fingers and you need all day. Practise with your mind and you will do as much in two hours.'

This is the essence of what psychologist Anders Ericsson discovered in his research on top performers. Widely

regarded as the world's 'expert on experts', Ericsson's research inspired books such as *The Talent Code* and *Talent Is Overrated*, which explain that experts don't become world-class in their respective fields because they're smarter or more talented but, rather, because they spend years engaging in more effective methods of practice than their peers.

For instance, in a 2001 basketball study (Cleary & Zimmerman) researchers videotaped 43 basketball players as they practised shooting free throws while describing their thought process out loud for the camera.

> 66 The best practisers appear to approach practising differently. 99

When the researchers reviewed the practice footage, they observed two key differences in the practice habits of the best (70% success rate or higher) and worst (55% or lower) free-throw shooters.

The best free-throw shooters had specific goals about what they intended to focus on in each practice attempt: for instance, 'I'm going to keep my elbows in'.

The worst free-throw shooters, on the other hand, tended to have more general goals – such as 'Use good form'.

How the players responded to missed shots revealed another key difference in their practice. When the best shooters missed, they didn't just try again, but

Pitch perfect: musicians can learn from a 2001 study of basketball players, which found that having in mind specific goals before each free throw – rather than rote repetition – improved performance

first engaged in a thoughtful reflection process, attributing their miss to a specific technical problem – such as 'I didn't bend my knees'. This led to a clearer goal for the next practice attempt and, ultimately, a deeper and more refined understanding of the skill with which each free-throw attempt should be executed, whether it was a make or a miss.

Conversely, the worst shooters were more likely to attribute missed free throws to non-specific factors, like 'My rhythm was off' or 'I wasn't focused'. While these explanations may have been true, they did little to inform the players' next practice attempt or to help evolve their understanding of the underlying mechanics of a successful free throw.

So what might this process look like for musicians?

While a less-effective practiser might passively repeat a passage over and over until it starts to sound better, effective practisers engage in a more active problem-solving process.

Consider a violinist who is troubleshooting a passage that isn't consistently in tune. After playing through the passage, they might start by thinking through a series of questions such as 'OK … which note was out of tune? Was it flat or sharp? By how much? What might have caused this?'

They might then respond by thinking, 'Hmmm … the G sharp in bar 3 was slightly flat. I think this happened because my thumb was squeezing the neck of the instrument, my first finger didn't lighten up enough during the shift, and I didn't bring my elbow around soon enough.'

This might be followed by 'Given all of this … let me see what happens when I lift up with my left hand, prepare my elbow and left hand slightly in advance of the shift, avoid clamping down on the instrument with my chin, and release tension in my left shoulder as well.'

It may take several cycles of experimentation for the musician to identify the exact combination of variables that produces the desired result, so repetition plays a part in this type of practice as well. The difference is that there is more explicit thinking, planning, and reflecting associated with each repetition, which leads to more concrete and permanent solutions.

Ericsson called this 'deliberate practice'. And studies across a range of different performance domains – from music to sports, chess, surgery and more – suggest that top performers tend to engage in this type of practice more consistently than less-expert performers.

Of course, it's not just a performer's technical accuracy or beautiful sound that makes a performance memorable. It's the feeling of effortlessness, spontaneity and risk that gives us goosebumps and makes a performance truly special.

This too takes a certain type of practice. Because, as calm and collected as great performers often appear onstage, the reality is that they often experience some of the same butterflies and nerves that the rest of us do, no matter how many years or decades of experience they've had in the spotlight.

When the adrenaline kicks in, the instinctive human response is to become more risk-averse and to play it safe. However, giving in to this impulse only leads to dull, uninspired and careful performances – which is no more enjoyable for the performer than it is for the listener.

So how do top performers prepare themselves for this inevitability?

Pianist Claudio Arrau was once asked if his teacher, Martin Krause (a student of virtuoso pianist-composer Franz Liszt), had any special teaching methods. According to Arrau, Krause believed that, to communicate a sense of effortless mastery to the audience, one had to cultivate 'reserves of technique' during practice: a process that required practising the most difficult sections of a piece at different speeds, in different rhythms, with a wider range of dynamics and articulations and in different keys. He even practised playing sections with large leaps or skips with his eyes closed.

Many other musicians have spoken to the value of integrating this kind of variability into one's practice. For instance, violinist Pamela Frank has encouraged students not only to practise their solo repertoire with 1,000% expression, but to practise scales expressively as well. Her rationale being, 'If you've practised mechanically, you'll play mechanically. If you treat a scale like a great melody, when it shows

up in the Beethoven concerto, it will be a great melody.'

Similarly, violist Toby Appel has said that he doesn't practise all the things he's going to do onstage so much as he practises all the things that he *might* do onstage.

Though these are just a few examples, they suggest that experienced performers may be intuitively aware of a learning strategy known as 'variable practice' in the motor-learning literature.

In a seminal 1978 study (Kerr & Booth), researchers compared two groups of 8-year-olds who practised tossing beanbags to targets at various distances for several weeks. One group practised on a target three feet away, while the other group practised with targets placed two and four feet away.

At the end of the study, when the children were tested on their ability to hit the three-foot target, the ones who had practised from two and four feet – and never from three feet – actually demonstrated significantly greater accuracy than those who practised at three feet the entire time.

Subsequent studies have reinforced this finding, suggesting that practising a skill repeatedly in exactly the same way can create the illusion of rapid learning, but lead to skills that are more fragile and less reliable when the situation changes – such as when your hands are cold or sweaty, or the conductor pushes the tempo slightly faster than they did in rehearsals, the action of the piano keys

Hungarian virtuoso Leopold Auer, who told his students: 'Practise with your fingers and you need all day. Practise with your mind and you will do as much in two hours.'

❝ To play in tune you have to listen really, really carefully. One of the most helpful lessons I was ever taught was to just get one or two notes unbelievably in tune, so they have that ringing, shining and glowing quality to them. Once you know what that feels like, it's almost something that you can get addicted to, and you want everything you play to have that same ringing quality to it. So just focus on those one or two notes … and get that ringing quality, and your ears will start to demand more of the same.

Violinist Nicola Benedetti's advice on how to practise playing in tune, in one of her YouTube videos

is much heavier than the instrument you practised on, or the acoustics of the hall demand that you project your sound further into the space than when playing in your living room.

In other words, when the goal is to play one's best not just in the practice room but onstage as well, experienced performers and researchers appear to have arrived at the same conclusion: that practising subtle variations of a passage can more effectively facilitate an optimal performance than putting in dozens of identical repetitions.

What's fascinating is that this approach to practising has benefits for the listener as well as the performer.

In a study conducted at Arizona State University (Langer et al., 2009), 60 members of the college orchestra were asked to perform the last movement of Brahms's Symphony No. 1 twice.

For one of the performances, the researchers asked the orchestra to 'think about the finest performance of this piece that you can remember, and play it that way'. The idea was to give the musicians a clear but relatively passive goal that was oriented more around replicating an ideal than creating something new in the moment.

In the other performance, the musicians were asked to 'play this piece in the finest manner you can, offering subtle new nuances to your performance'. The researchers' intention here was to frame the directive as a more active goal

that might encourage the musicians to be more creative, spontaneous and improvisational.

The musicians reported having more fun in the 'subtle nuances' version of the performance, but – in order to see if an audience might discern any meaningful differences between the two performances – 143 community choir members were asked to listen to both recordings and to report if they had a preference between the two versions.

The vast majority of listeners – 88% – did in fact express a preference. And 83% of those with a preference preferred the more dynamic, improvisational, 'subtle nuances' performance.

I once read an anecdote about the violinist Isaac Stern, who was approached by a fan following a performance, exclaiming: 'I would give my life to play like you!' To which Stern replied, 'That I did.'

The reality of what it takes to perform at a world-class level may not be quite as dramatic as Stern's response implies. Yet I hope that this tiny glimpse into a musician's practice does help to illustrate that the ease with which our favourite artists create transcendently beautiful moments onstage is not merely the product of talent and repetition, but the result of a much richer and more fascinatingly complex constellation of practice strategies than the phrase 'Practice, practice, practice' might suggest! ●

Noa Kageyama was a student violinist at the Juilliard School before becoming a performance coach. He has contributed to numerous papers and he blogs under the name Bulletproof Musician.

EDINBURGH INTERNATIONAL FESTIVAL

5–28 August

CELEBRATING 75 YEARS OF BRINGING WORLD CULTURES TOGETHER

CZECH PHILHARMONIC LONDON SYMPHONY ORCHESTRA
THE PHILADELPHIA ORCHESTRA **BERGEN PHILHARMONIC ORCHESTRA**
PHILHARMONIA HELSINKI PHILHARMONIC ORCHESTRA **THE ENGLISH CONCERT**

ZUBIN MEHTA **VÍKINGUR ÓLAFSSON** YANNICK NÉZET-SÉGUIN **ELIM CHAN**
MALIN BYSTRÖM IESTYN DAVIES **GOLDA SCHULTZ** SUSANNA MÄLKKI
NICOLA BENEDETTI **ANNE SOFIE VON OTTER** BRUCE LIU

RUSALKA SAUL **SALOME** CARMINA BURANA

AND MANY MORE

eif.co.uk
#edintfest

Charity No SC004694

·EDINBVRGH·
THE CITY OF EDINBURGH COUNCIL

CREATIVE SCOTLAND
ALBA | CHRUTHACHAIL

A World
of Music

George Walker overcame racial prejudice to become
one of the most performed – and most decorated –
American composers of the 20th century. As the
Proms celebrates his centenary, his son, **IAN WALKER**,
reflects on a musical output inseparable from the
world in which it was conceived

In 2017, the year before my father died, we sat down for an informal interview for our family archives. As he frequently did, he said something seemingly incongruous. 'I never thought I could be a composer,' he announced, his voice at 95 years old thick with gravel. 'It was not something I expected to be.' I was taken aback by this sense of surprise. Examined in retrospect, his life argued the opposite. He began to study the piano at the age of 5. I say 'study' because I don't believe anything was done lightly in the Walker household. His father had emigrated from Jamaica at the age of 14 without family or prospects for work. After shovelling coal into home furnaces for a winter, he put himself through medical school and became a successful doctor, owning several homes in Washington DC.

The same level of uncompromising grit was sanded into everything in the Walker home. Early to bed and early to rise, the Walker household was bustling by 6.00am, even on Saturdays. Maths and English lessons would interrupt playtime in summer, as young George's mother sat him and *all* the neighbourhood kids down for class (I suffered the same fate at my father's hands, some 40 years later). Her teachings paid off: George was allowed to graduate directly from the 4th to the 7th grade at the age of 9. In junior high (now aged 11) he began studying music

◀ George Walker, captured at the piano by his son Ian; the composer's first career, as a concert pianist, was cut short by illness

at the Junior Department at Howard University, the youngest music student in his class. After graduating from Dunbar High School at 14 (by which time he was giving public concerts at Howard) George Walker enrolled in the Music Department at Oberlin University, Ohio. Then came Philadelphia's Curtis Institute of Music, where he studied with renowned pianist Rudolf Serkin, and a long line of 'firsts': in 1945 alone he became the first Black graduate of the Curtis Institute, the first Black pianist to perform a solo recital at New York's Town Hall, and the first Black soloist to perform with the Philadelphia Orchestra. That was also the year in which he composed *Lyric for Strings*, which became his most enduring and most popular work.

George Walker's progression as an artist appeared rapid and sure-footed. He studied composition with the famed Nadia Boulanger in Paris. She was so impressed with his work that she exempted him from her obligatory counterpoint and harmony lessons – a privilege she did not extend to fellow US composers Aaron Copland or Elliott Carter. In the 1950s Walker toured Europe as a pianist. He obtained a PhD from the Eastman School of Music in New York – again, the first Black student to do so – later to be complemented by seven honorary doctorates from various other institutions. He was inducted into the American Academy of Arts and Letters in 1999 and the American Classical Music Hall of Fame a year later. And, of course, there was a Pulitzer Prize for *Lilacs* in 1996.

To all appearances he seemed destined to become a composer. Perhaps, then, the surprise he expressed in our interview had more to do with the obstacles he faced, and the perception that serious classical music was beyond the 'mental capabilities' of Black Americans. The list of firsts that began in 1945 came well before the USA moved towards equality. It would be three years before the armed services were desegregated; nine years before Brown vs. Board of Education ended segregation in public schools and before the Civil Rights Movement got started; and 10 years before Rosa Parks famously refused to move to the back of a bus in Montgomery, Alabama.

Washington DC, where Walker was born in 1922, was known to be *relatively* free of Jim Crow segregation laws, but public schools were still segregated, as were recreational facilities. You could dine in any restaurant but – as he would describe years later at our kitchen table – there were separate lines for Blacks and Whites at the bank. While attending the Curtis Institute, however, he was taken aback at the level of racism in Philadelphia. He was frequently asked to leave restaurants and train cars and, on one occasion, was approached by an usher at the First Baptist Church who hissed, 'Why don't you go to your own church?' In the face of such harassment he did what many Black Americans did: ignored it and carried on with the business at hand.

In 1953, after returning from an eight-city concert tour of Europe, George Walker suffered a severe ulcer attack that required a month's recovery in hospital. When he emerged, he knew his career as a concert pianist was over. Though he continued to perform from time to time, and later produced several recordings, it would be years before his health fully returned. From that point on his focus turned to composition.

George Walker with his son Ian in 2017, the year before the composer's death aged 96

In his lifetime he composed over 90 works – pieces for orchestra, piano, wind ensemble, guitar, voice, organ, harp, percussion and brass. He claimed to be only interested in compositional excellence, eschewing musical trends, cultural identity and political statement. Yet the world at large was a frequent undercurrent in his work. The melancholic and hopeful *Lyric for Strings* was inspired by the death of his grandmother, an escaped slave, and the lush composition seems to follow her journey from bondage to freedom. His *Poem for Soprano and Chamber Ensemble* was written to draw attention to the problem of homelessness in America. *Foils for Orchestra* is a homage to Joseph Bologne, Chevalier de Saint-Georges, the 18th-century Black composer who was also a renowned fencer. *Lilacs* is a setting of Walt Whitman's *When lilacs last in the dooryard bloom'd*, a pastoral elegy following the assassination of Abraham Lincoln. Woven into the piece are elements of the African American spiritual 'Lil' boy, how old are you?' and musical memories of my father's childhood trips to the country (you can hear the melodic chatter of birds at the beginning of the last movement). Clearly Walker's heartstrings were pulled by current racial divisions and their sorrows – by harsh surrounding clouds, fallen stars and cruel hands. And – as with *Lyric for Strings* some 50 years earlier – a rising hope, free and tender and wild. ●

Ian Walker is a film-maker, playwright, actor, director and producer. Winner of the International Larry Corse Prize, the John Golden Prize and a Bay One Acts Festival Award for Best Play, he lives with his wife and two children in the San Francisco Bay Area.

Lancing College
Senior School & Sixth Form

Be inspired
Be brilliant
Be you

Music Scholarships and Exhibitions available

FIND OUT MORE
LANCINGCOLLEGE.CO.UK

**YOUR
INCREDIBLE
JOURNEY**

Registered Charity Number 1076483

Music & the Monarchy

Whether for entertainment at court, ceremonial occasions or solemn remembrance, music has been bound up with royal ritual for centuries, as JOHN GREENING observes in this Platinum Jubilee year of the Queen's accession to the throne

I f those trumpets discovered in Tutankhamun's tomb are any guide, the use of music in royal ceremonies is an ancient tradition. In Britain, certainly, it has long been a way of expressing the sovereign's authority – sometimes through sheer volume of sound – and channelling their mystery. Royalty and music, it seems, are equally enigmatic.

Many will think immediately of George Frideric Handel: the performances of his *Water Music* on the Thames (George I wanted it played three times) or the *Music for the Royal Fireworks* marking the end in 1748 of the now-forgotten War of the Austrian Succession. *Zadok the Priest*, too, comes to mind, with its stately opening arpeggios and repeated refrain of 'God Save the King', though the three other Coronation Anthems are equally sublime, transcending their original purpose as the finest ceremonial pieces do. Having dropped his umlaut and become more English than the English, the German-born Handel understood his role perfectly: help the Hanoverian monarchy sell the Act of Union. He can hardly have foreseen what a hit he would turn out to be, something beyond the reach of the earlier composers Queen Anne had encouraged, including William Croft and Jeremiah Clarke.

◀ The Dukes of York, Gloucester and Ireland at a feast with King Richard II, *c*1386: the lavish menu included 100 pounds of venison and 11,000 eggs – so required a fanfare *(top left)* to match

But before all these there had been Henry Purcell, a child prodigy who died too soon, prompting a verse eulogy from Dryden that imagined all the songbirds 'struck dumb' in awe of him: 'The Gods are pleas'd alone with Purcell's layes.' He had certainly pleased the monarchy, turning out flattering Odes to Charles II and, after the Glorious Revolution of 1688, an annual Birthday Ode to Mary. His music for the Queen's funeral (used at his own soon after) never fails to produce a shiver – that steady drumbeat and the searing brass.

Purcell was closely involved with the Chapel Royal – originally a peripatetic group of court priests and musicians, much envied by European monarchs – but also inherited the lively tradition of the masque. These were vast court spectacles, conceived on a grand scale by impresarios such as Inigo Jones, scripted by the likes of Ben Jonson. The librettos are fascinating to read but were only ever printed as a souvenir of the event, so all stage directions are in the past tense. Over a hundred were staged during the early years of the Stuarts, including the *Entertainment at Althorp* to welcome James I from Scotland. What made masques unique was the active participation of members of the court and royal family. Music was central, with songs and formal dances woven into the action, but the names of composers and performers were seldom considered important enough to record (rather as musical credits whizz by on a modern movie screen).

Looking back yet further, it's surprising that, although Elizabeth I fostered some

of the greatest composers, they are remembered more for melancholy song (Dowland) and spiritual choral reflections (Byrd) than for great public outpourings. Nevertheless, the premiere of Tallis's 40-part motet *Spem in alium (see Prom 50)* – possibly for the Queen's 40th birthday – must have caused a stir. Elizabeth inherited a love of music from her father, Henry VIII, enjoying grand musical accompaniments to her banquets (12 trumpets and 12 kettledrums for one at Greenwich) and during royal progresses (at Kenilworth, a 'delectable harmony of hautbois, shawms, cornets').

Henry himself may not have written 'Greensleeves', and tyrants do like to claim authorship of anything popular, yet there were always sweet sounds at his court: it was a lute player there, after all, who attracted Anne Boleyn. Henry also used music to impress rivals. The Field of Cloth of Gold was a spectacular summit (with jousting and crumpets!) where the French king, Francis I, had his ears seduced or perhaps assaulted by Robert Fayrfax, William Cornysh – and, naturally, Henry Tudor. There was even a kind of battle of the respective choirs and organs, alternating between French and English forces.

All of which brings us to Agincourt and back again, accompanied by a certain battle song, familiar from William Walton's soundtrack to Olivier's *Henry V*. Walton is more convincing than most recent composers in ceremonial mode (think of the marches *Crown Imperial* and *Orb and Sceptre*, or indeed the regal

The Queen seated at the Chair of Estate after entering Westminster Abbey to the strains of Parry's anthem *I was glad* at her Coronation on 2 June 1953

The Kingdom Choir and *(centre)* conductor Karen Gibson at St George's Chapel, Windsor Castle, after singing 'Stand By Me' at the wedding of Prince Harry and Meghan Markle on 19 May 2018

savagery of *Belshazzar's Feast*), maybe because, despite his jazzy exterior, he shared a sense of occasion with the Victorians. Much modern royal music has a taproot in the 19th century. Prince Albert was very musical, and Mendelssohn often visited, performing at Buckingham Palace, where the Prince Consort installed a splendid new organ. But the real renaissance in English music was about to happen further up the road, at the Royal College of Music. Its director, Charles Hubert Parry, is little discussed today, though Prince Charles presented a fascinating TV programme about the composer. Parry's music is often elegiac (as it happens, he died in the 1918 Spanish flu pandemic), but he could also make joy sound genuine. The anthem *I was glad*, with its cry of 'Vivat regina!', is a coronation fixture; and his setting of Blake's *Jerusalem* needs no introduction.

Yet, asked to describe a typical royal 'sound', we'd probably not select Parry or Walton. Rather – much as Copland evokes American open spaces – it is Edward Elgar's *nobilmente* mood that conjures archetypal royal magnificence. Of course, music written to order doesn't always succeed. Elgar's 'Pomp and Circumstantial' genius stumbled in some of his lesser-known marches. Arnold Bax, however, even when burnt out as a symphonist, produced for Princess Elizabeth and Philip's wedding in 1947 a set of impressively symphonic 'raucous fanfares'. As with Poets Laureate, some Masters of the King's (or Queen's) Music are barely remembered – or at least not

for their royal contributions. Walter Parratt (1841–1924) held the post under three monarchs, but is associated with one thing: a poem he commissioned for Elgar's *Coronation Ode*. It's unlikely that Edward VII himself suggested recycling the 'tune that will knock 'em flat', but A. C. Benson definitely provided the words – 'Land of Hope and Glory' – now a staple of the Last Night of the Proms.

> 66 The use of music in royal ceremonies has long been a way of expressing the sovereign's authority, and channelling their mystery. 99

Precisely what will hit the mark at a grand ceremony is hard to predict. Ralph Vaughan Williams was very pragmatic about such pieces, but while his *Serenade to Music* for Proms founder-conductor Henry Wood's Jubilee Concert is often revived, *Flourish for a Coronation* is not. Benjamin Britten also felt music should be useful, but there were misjudgements, as when the Japanese government rejected his piece commissioned for the 2,600th anniversary of the Japanese Empire (the *Sinfonia da Requiem*, with movement titles from the Requiem Mass), not to mention the disastrous premiere of his coronation opera, *Gloriana*, depicting an ageing, lonely Elizabeth I. As Britten's biographer Neil Powell puts it, the applause 'was muted not only because so many hands were elegantly gloved'.

Yet the musicologist Hans Keller thought it perhaps his finest opera. Britten also left us one of the most effective arrangements of *God Save the Queen*.

Much festive occasional music is played once, then forgotten. How often has Arthur Bliss's cantata *Shield of Faith* for the quincentenary of St George's Chapel, Windsor, been heard since 1975? Or anything he and Grace Williams and Alun Hoddinott composed for the 1969 Investiture of Prince Charles? However, revivals do happen. Elizabeth Maconchy's coronation overture *Proud Thames* (1953) made the 2019 Proms.

But it is the elegies that tend to endure, and sometimes they arrive unexpectedly. Paul Hindemith's *Trauermusik*, for example, was written when he learnt of the death of George V, and the BBC Symphony Orchestra gave its premiere the very next day, with the composer as viola soloist. At the funeral of Diana, Princess of Wales, when a nation's grief urgently needed an outlet, there was Elton John's 'Candle in the Wind', there was 'I Vow to Thee, My Country' and there was John Tavener's *Song for Athene*. At such times, our needs are no different from those who attended Queen Mary's funeral over three centuries ago. Purcell's drumbeats still sound down the centuries. ●

Poet and critic John Greening is the editor of several anthologies, including *Accompanied Voices: Poets on Composers from Thomas Tallis to Arvo Pärt*. He has collaborated with the composers Roderick Williams, Philip Lancaster and Cecilia McDowall.

Music for Royal Occasions
PROM 10 • 22 JULY

The Rhythm of a Reign

Jennie Bond looks back at the music that has underscored the Queen's 70 years as monarch

Sometimes only the power of music can define the significance of certain moments in royal history. The sadness of the whole country when Diana, Princess of Wales, died in 1997 was so completely captured at her funeral by Sir Elton John. Nearly quarter of a century later, it was a solitary piper who caught the mood at the Duke of Edinburgh's scaled-back funeral last year with 'Flowers of the Forest' as the Queen watched her husband being laid to rest.

In my travels reporting on the Royal Family over the past 30 years, I have seen them enjoy – and occasionally endure – endless concerts and musical performances. Sometimes these events did, indeed, seem endless. I remember a visit to Winnipeg, Canada, when the Queen and Duke, noses red with cold, doggedly sat through what felt like an interminable cultural display of music and dance. At the end of each song, the Queen would hopefully reach down for the handbag at her feet, ready for a polite exit, just as yet another melody began. Back went the handbag, up sat the Queen and on went the show.

But the music of each country visited by the royals is part and parcel of a tour, just as key events of the royal calendar are marked by music. The Changing of the Guard ceremony at Buckingham Palace is unthinkable without the Bands of the Household Division, which have always played a mix of traditional and popular music. It is said that on one occasion in 1920 the band was playing an excerpt from a popular operetta when a footman arrived with a message from King George V for the Director of Music. It read: 'His Majesty does not know what the band has just played, but it is never to be played again.'

We can only imagine what the Queen made of the opening to the Party at the Palace to celebrate her Golden Jubilee in 2002. I remember shivers running down my spine as former Queen guitarist, Brian May, stood on the palace roof and electrifyingly played the National Anthem. Ten years later it was the band Madness who clambered up onto the palace roof to sing 'Our House', to mark the Queen's Diamond Jubilee. Moments like that show the monarchy can move with the times.

There is, though, something that stirs the soul about the traditional beat of the massed bands at the annual Trooping the Colour spectacle. I am far from a traditionalist myself, but I defy anyone to watch and hear those bands march by without stomping their feet in time with the music. It is the rhythm that has marked the Queen's 70-year reign.

But perhaps the rhythm of her heart is still the song from *Oklahoma!* believed to have been the favourite of the young Princess and her handsome suitor, Philip of Greece, all those years ago, before their romance was public knowledge. Their song, it is said, was 'People Will Say We're in Love'. And they were. Until the very end.

Broadcaster and journalist Jennie Bond was the BBC's Royal Correspondent from 1989 to 2003.

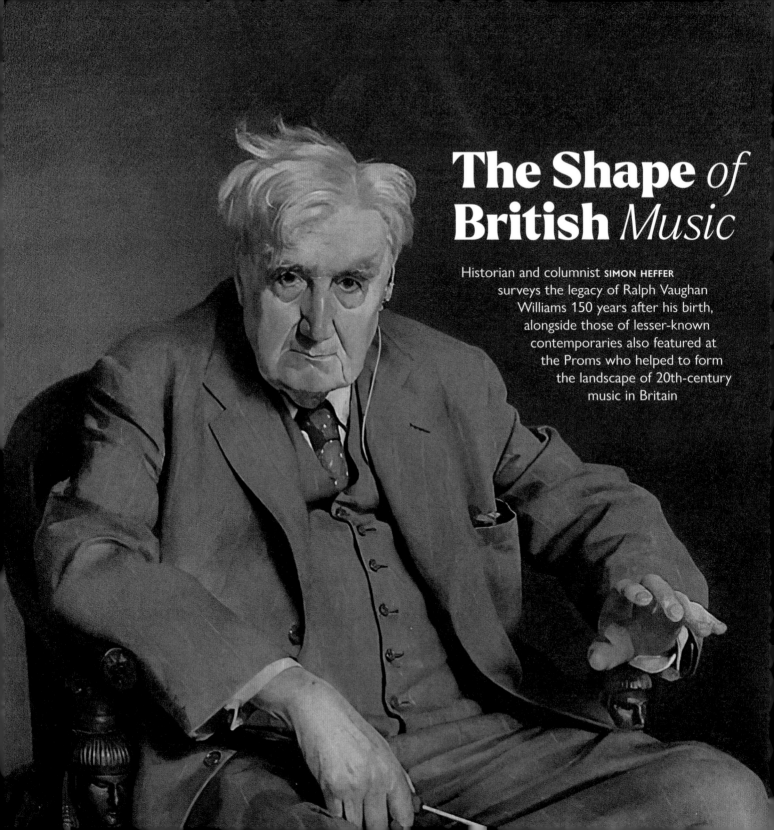

The Shape *of* British *Music*

Historian and columnist SIMON HEFFER surveys the legacy of Ralph Vaughan Williams 150 years after his birth, alongside those of lesser-known contemporaries also featured at the Proms who helped to form the landscape of 20th-century music in Britain

Cultural history is stuffed with paradoxes, and in British musical life one of the greatest must surely be the publication, in 1904, of Oskar Schmitz's unpleasant anti-English essay *Das Land ohne Musik* ('The Land Without Music'). There is some doubt that Schmitz himself coined the phrase, which had been uttered by Germans for at least the preceding 35 years when they wished to denigrate Britain by suggesting it was a cultural backwater. But for Schmitz to launch his polemic just at the moment when the profession of music in the British Isles – whether composers or performers – was bursting into life was a case either of bad timing or of prejudice blinding someone to reality. Also, the British public seemed to have an insatiable appetite for classical music – which was not least why, nine years before Schmitz's article, Henry Wood had co-founded the Promenade Concerts, then held every summer in London's Queen's Hall.

So greatly had music flourished in late Victorian and Edwardian Britain that, just as Schmitz went into print, Edward Elgar was knighted for his achievements. Coming, it seemed, from nowhere – in fact from his father's music shop in Worcester – Elgar had in the preceding

◀ Vaughan Williams shortly before his death (painting by Gerald Kelly, 1879–1972); the hearing aid was one of several he used beginning in his seventies, the largest of which he referred to as his 'coffee pot'

few years become a household name, winning fame with the 'Enigma' Variations, *The Dream of Gerontius*, his *Coronation Ode* and – an indispensable feature of the Proms – his *Pomp and Circumstance* March No. 1. He had become the foremost composer of the English musical renaissance, as it became widely known, a 'New Wave' of composers considered to have started in the early 1880s with the first works of Hubert Parry and Charles Villiers Stanford. In the first half of the 20th century, Britain became a force in classical music for the first time since the era of Purcell; it became the land *with* music.

Three British composers featured at this year's Proms exemplify the progress of the nation's music, and the growth in its popularity, between the late 19th and mid-20th centuries. The most notable is Ralph Vaughan Williams, a pupil of Parry and Stanford, born 150 years ago this year; but there is also his predecessor, Ethel Smyth (1858–1944), whose formidable talent and personality ensured she did not suffer the high degree of prejudice that harmed the chances of many other aspiring composers who did not happen to be men; and Doreen Carwithen, born a century ago and who, following the trail blazed for women by Ethel Smyth, made a reputation in the mid-20th century not only as an orchestral composer but also as a prodigious writer of film music.

Ethel Smyth was a pioneering composer who studied at the Leipzig Conservatory in the 1870s and was heavily influenced

by the music of Wagner and Berlioz. Typical of her deeply critical and radical approach to the study of music, she left Leipzig after just a year out of dissatisfaction with the quality of the teaching. However, while there, she met Tchaikovsky, Dvořák and Brahms and, while steeping herself in the European classical tradition, also began to develop a distinctive voice of her own. On returning to England, she worked closely with Arthur Sullivan, a fellow composer who shared her European influences, and who was the first of several British men to champion her work.

> 66 Vaughan Williams would have an overwhelming effect on British musical life and would come to enjoy a posthumous reputation of towering proportions. 99

In Ethel Smyth's lifetime, some critics made the absurd complaint about her music that it appeared too masculine for a woman to have written: clearly, that said more about the peculiar mindset of the critics than it did about her abilities. Yet Dame Ethel (as she would become in 1922, the first woman so honoured for her music) wrote a range of works of subtlety and inventiveness, from chamber music very much in the style of the European masters to her masterpiece, the opera *The Wreckers*, for which she eventually secured a performance in Leipzig in 1906. Yet it was not until 1909 that she

Ethel Smyth (top) and Doreen Carwithen, two of the figures who contributed to the English musicial renaissance in the first part of the 20th century

managed to have the work performed in Britain, thanks to her friend and staunch advocate Thomas Beecham; the recognition she won spurred her on to further creativity. However, her political activism meant her music had to be put aside for a time: she was a powerful figure in the women's suffrage movement, and it is even claimed she fell in love with Emmeline Pankhurst, one of the movement's key agitators. She did, though, write *The March of the Women*, the anthem of the suffragettes, and went to prison in Holloway for two months for breaking a window at the home of the Colonial Secretary, Lewis Harcourt. She was released because the prison doctor regarded her as unstable and a hysteric. The evidence of the rest of her life suggests that no diagnosis could have been further from the truth. Her time in Holloway may have influenced her last major work, a choral symphony entitled *The Prison*, which she wrote in 1930, although its first recording was only released in 2020: it features a dialogue between a condemned prisoner and his soul, and the recording earned Dame Ethel acclaim that was decades overdue.

Doreen Carwithen's musical career and life were less dramatic, but recognition for her has, as with many British composers male and female of the early and mid-20th century, been slow to come. She started to compose in the late 1930s while still at school, and won a scholarship to the Royal Academy of Music. There, she played the cello in a string quartet and began a lifelong association with William

Alwyn, who taught her harmony and, later, composition. She would marry him in 1975 after years as his amanuensis and secretary. Alwyn himself wrote the scores for over 70 films, and his pupil would follow him in that genre, being specially trained to do so by the RAM. But Doreen Carwithen – who preferred to be known by her second name of Mary – also enjoyed the patronage of Adrian Boult when, as a young woman of 25, he performed her overture *ODTAA* (One Damn Thing After Another) with the London Philharmonic Orchestra. Critics said it showed the influence of E. J. Moeran, another product of the English musical renaissance, whose wife Peers Coetmore had taught Carwithen the cello. It certainly has close kinship with the Anglo-Irish composer's idiom, and exudes energy, melody and verve. In 1948 it was followed by her sumptuous Concerto for Piano and Strings. Sadly, it was not until after the death of her husband in 1985 that her own talent as a composer began to be recognised properly, and her reputation is bound to grow yet.

The re-emergence of classical music as a cornerstone of British cultural life had been happening gradually since the 1870s, when Smyth and Elgar were making their first attempts to write music, and Arthur Sullivan was already famous for his collaborations with W. S. Gilbert. But the development of British music was turbocharged by the foundation in 1882, on the initiative of George Grove, of the Royal College of Music. Over the next few decades this new conservatoire would produce some of the greatest composers in the country's history. One would be Ralph Vaughan Williams, who went to the RCM in 1890 and came under the influence of Parry and Stanford, the two leading academics appointed by Grove.

Vaughan Williams would have an overwhelming effect on British musical life until his death in 1958, and would (after the near-statutory period of neglect that almost every British composer seems to face after his or her death) come to enjoy a posthumous reputation of towering proportions. His impact was not merely as the composer of nine symphonies, numerous orchestral works, four operas, several concertos, cantatas and song-cycles. He led the development of what he called a 'national music', to liberate British composers from following the idiom of the German greats, and so countering his teacher, Parry, with his often-professed homage to Brahms. He sought to craft this uniquely British voice by collecting folk songs in the early years of the 20th century. He did so along with Cecil Sharp, Gustav Holst and George Butterworth. This was a visionary activity: none of them could have known the Great War was coming, but all recognised that society was changing from a predominantly rural to a predominantly urban one, and that the old traditions of folk-singing were fast dying out. When the war did come, it inevitably severed some cultural links with the past, and confirmed that their collection of folk songs happened just in time.

Scarcely less important than Vaughan Williams's contribution as a composer

A Very British Bond

Jenny Doctor outlines the relationship between Vaughan Williams and the BBC

Vaughan Williams with Larry Adler before the London premiere of the composer's *Romance* for harmonica and orchestra at the Proms in 1952

When the BBC was formed in 1922, Vaughan Williams was already aged 50 and well established. His influence would soon also spread via BBC radio. He worked closely with the BBC throughout the 1920s, including after the Corporation took over the Promenade Concerts in 1927.

In 1930 Adrian Boult was appointed BBC Director of Music and Chief Conductor of the new BBC Symphony Orchestra. Boult already had a strong working relationship with Vaughan Williams, and the BBC competed for opportunities to give his first performances and invited him to conduct in broadcasts. He conducted at least once in most Proms seasons for over 20 years.

At the start of the Second World War Vaughan Williams encouraged the BBC to step up. 'When so many people are looking for comfort & encouragement from music … surely we ought to give them something that will grip.' He gave talks encouraging active music-making and promoted marching tunes 'with real

blood in their veins'. In 1944 the BBC asked him for a victory anthem and, months before war's end, *Thanksgiving for Victory* was pre-recorded 'for immediate use when the moment comes'.

Vaughan Williams's 75th birthday in October 1947 may represent the height of his renown with the BBC. A retrospective of best-known recorded works was aired, and broadcast concerts featured major works. The birthday itself included friends' tributes, while Boult's homage to 'the undisputed leader of English musical life' was recorded in three languages and heard across BBC European Services.

After Boult left the BBC in 1950, contact with Vaughan Williams was less personal. Yet his morality opera, *The Pilgrim's Progress*, was broadcast in the 1951 Festival of Britain, and most or all of his symphonies to date were given in the 1951 and 1952 Proms seasons. The Coronation Concert in 1953 included *A Sea Symphony* (No. 1) and, although at first uncertain about broadcasting the premiere of the *Sinfonia antartica* (No. 7), the BBC asked if Vaughan Williams might talk about it. 'All my life I have refused to talk about my own music,' he replied, 'and I'm certainly not going to start at 80.' In early 1955 all seven symphonies were aired. The first performances of Symphonies No. 8 (1956) and No. 9 (1958) were broadcast and the two works were later heard at the Proms. The latter Prom was attended by the composer, three weeks before his death.

In a eulogy Boult wrote of values underlying not only their friendship, but the collaboration between composer and Corporation: 'He was like many great men, approachable, sympathetic and of a piercing integrity.'

Jenny Doctor is the author of *The BBC and Ultra-Modern Music, 1922–1936* (CUP, 1999) and co-editor of *The Proms: A New History* (Thames & Hudson, 2007). She is a Professor and Library Head at the University of Cincinnati.

Wenlock Edge in Shropshire, after which Vaughan Williams named his settings of poems from A. E. Housman's *A Shropshire Lad*; the cycle's pastoral lyricism is far removed from the fierce expression of the Fourth Symphony, written 25 years later, between the wars

and musicologist was his role as a teacher and encourager of new talent. He enthusiastically praised Doreen Carwithen's First String Quartet (1945), one of her most accomplished works and one that reminds the listener how sad it was that she wrote relatively little music because of her devoted work for her husband for many years. Largely through his work at the RCM, where he taught composition for 20 years between the wars, Vaughan Williams had a direct influence as teacher or mentor on Moeran, Arthur Bliss, Gordon Jacob, Stanley Bate, Elizabeth Maconchy (possibly the most accomplished woman composer Britain has yet produced) and Grace Williams. In 1910 Herbert Howells, then 17 years old, heard the first performance in Gloucester Cathedral of Vaughan Williams's *Fantasia on a Theme by Thomas Tallis*, and it changed his life, making him resolve to become a composer.

Vaughan Williams remained a strong influence on Howells, who also taught at the RCM, for the rest of his life. When Howells was reluctant to let his masterpiece *Hymnus Paradisi* be premiered at the 1950 Three Choirs Festival because of its intensely personal nature (it was written to express his grief at the death in 1935 of his 9-year-old son Michael), it was Vaughan Williams who persuaded him to relent. He had a formidable effect on Howells's considerable output of church music – an irony given that both men at various times considered themselves atheists. Yet there was possibly no composer on whom Vaughan Williams had a greater influence than Gerald Finzi, whom he met in the late 1920s and by whom he was adopted as a mentor. Vaughan Williams found Finzi a job teaching at the Royal Academy of Music in the 1930s, and acted as a consultant on many of Finzi's works, just as Gustav Holst had done for Vaughan Williams – the two men had met at the RCM in the 1890s. Through his role as a teacher and *éminence grise*, Vaughan Williams did more than anyone to shape the landscape of British music in the first half of the 20th century.

After the deaths of Elgar, Holst and Delius in 1934 Vaughan Williams became the undisputed leader of the profession of music in Britain, being admitted to the Order of Merit the following year. His name was also brought before a wider public in the 1940s by his film scores.

Vaughan Williams's relationship with folk song and the English pastoral tradition had coloured his reputation. His *Pastoral Symphony* (No. 3), first performed in 1922, was dismissed by one observer as 'VW rolling over and over in a ploughed field on a muddy day'; and Peter Warlock likened it to 'a cow looking over a gate'. It is a reputation made by the collecting of folk songs and by a few much-loved works, mainly from before the First World War, but represents only a fraction of him. He served throughout the war and saw its horrors first hand, and much music he wrote after it had an intrinsic darkness that owes more to his experience of the Western Front than to the bucolicism of the English countryside. The *Pastoral Symphony* depicts the landscape of France, not of England, though the composer was reluctant to discuss his feelings and inspiration in detail. It set the tone for what might best be termed Vaughan Williams's 'middle period'. His oratorio *Sancta civitas* of 1923–5 exudes reflectiveness and sobriety; his Piano Concerto of 1926–31 is percussive and alternates serenity with aggression. The same is true of his contemporaneous work *Job: A Masque for Dancing*, whose evocations of Satan are more earthly than other-worldly; but the apogee of this theme of anti-pastoralism is most clearly evoked between the wars by his Fourth Symphony, first performed by the BBC Symphony Orchestra under Adrian Boult in 1935.

The Fourth Symphony is a work of almost unrelenting anger and dissonance, unlike anything the composer had ever written.

He said after its premiere: 'I don't know whether I like it, but it's what I meant.' Why he meant what he meant has been much debated. He began the work at the time of the rise of Hitler. With the shadow of a second war looming over Britain, the Fourth Symphony was heard as an expression of rage by a composer who, having witnessed war at close quarters, was determined there should not be another one. However, Vaughan Williams's widow Ursula would say with apparent seriousness that the Fourth Symphony was inspired by his rage at the proposed siting of the Dorking bypass, near where he had then lived. This is a charming but unlikely story. As with his *Pastoral Symphony*, Vaughan Williams – like most Englishmen of his class and generation – was reluctant to discuss matters touching his deepest emotions.

He took the same approach to his Sixth Symphony, premiered in 1948, again by the BBC SO and Boult, and shaped by the experience of another terrible war. Critics said the final movement, played with an unrelieved *pianissimo*, echoed the nuclear holocaust of Hiroshima and Nagasaki. Vaughan Williams brushed that aside by citing Prospero's words from *The Tempest* – 'We are such stuff/ As dreams are made on, and our little life/ Is rounded with a sleep.' Yet there is also evidence that the saxophone solo in the aggressive Scherzo is the composer's tribute to Ken 'Snakehips' Johnson, who was killed in March 1941 when a landmine was dropped on the Café de Paris in London's West End.

This symphony seemed to get war out of his system. The music of his last decade (he died in 1958) became more serene, though there is an expansive sense of contemplation in his ninth and final symphony, first performed four months before his death. On his death his greatness was lauded, not least at his funeral in Westminster Abbey. And the end of his life marked the beginning of an enduring legend. ●

Simon Heffer's books include studies of composers and historians, including Vaughan Williams. He is a columnist for *The Sunday Telegraph* and a Professorial Research Fellow at the University of Buckingham.

Fantasia on a Theme by Thomas Tallis
PROM 2 • 16 JULY

Symphony No. 4
PROM 6 • 19 JULY

Silence and Music
PROM 10 • 22 JULY

A Sea Symhony (Symphony No. 1)
PROM 16 • 27 JULY

Rhosymeadre; Variations for brass band
PROM 32 • 9 AUGUST

Oboe Concerto
PROM 37 • 14 AUGUST

Tuba Concerto
PROM 39 • 15 AUGUST

The Lark Ascending
PROM 52 • 26 AUGUST

Four Last Songs
PROMS AT BIRMINGHAM • 29 AUGUST

See Index of Works for pieces by Ethel Smyth and Doreen Carwithen

"Churches are such heavenly buildings. Your legacy will help keep them flourishing on earth."

rian Blessed, Actor, Writer and Presenter

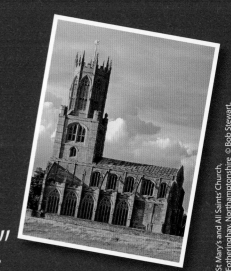

St Mary's and All Saints' Church, Fotheringhay, Northamptonshire © Bob Stewart.

ADORE CHURCH BUILDINGS. They're hauntingly beautiful, vocative and stir such powerful emotions. And they've always layed an important part in my life.

ut time takes its toll on all of us and churches are no exception. Many are threatened with leaking roofs, crumbling stonework nd the consequences of repeated closures during the andemic.

Churches have been key places for local communities during Covid-19, but once they are gone, they'll be gone forever.

Last year, gifts in Wills enabled the National Churches Trust to help remove 17 historic churches from Historic England's At Risk register.

A legacy from you can help save even more.

o find out more call Claire Walker on **020 7222 0605,** email: **legacy@nationalchurchestrust.org,** visit: **nationalchurchestrust.org/legacy** or complete the coupon below.

NATIONAL CHURCHES TRUST

Yours for good.

☐ Please send me details about leaving a legacy to the National Churches Trust. (Please affix a stamp.)

PG - 22

tle Forename Surname

ddress Postcode

eturn to Claire Walker, National Churches Trust, 7 Tufton Street London SW1P 3QB.

ease see our privacy policy at www.nationalchurchestrust.org/privacy as to how we hold your data securely nd privately. You will not be added to our mailing list and we will only use your details to send you this specific formation. Registered Charity Number: 1119845

Registered with FUNDRAISING REGULATOR

Courageous

Join us now at an open event
habsboys.org.uk & habsgirls.org.uk

Habs
HABERDASHERS'
BOYS' SCHOOL

Habs
HABERDASHERS'
GIRLS' SCHOOL

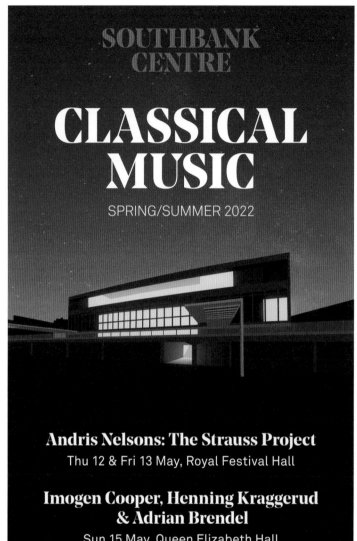

The Opera Doctor Will See You Now

Ahead of a season featuring three complete operas, as well as a project combining operatic works by Philip Glass and Handel, comedian CHRIS ADDISON performs a thorough examination of this oft-misunderstood art form

A h! Come in! Do sit down. Just move the Viking helmet off that chair. Don't know why it's there. They get everywhere. Welcome to the Opera Surgery, where we aim to answer any and every question you might have about the world's greatest art form. So. Fire away!

OK. What is opera?

Starting with the hard ones, eh? Basically, an opera is a story set to music. It's like going to the theatre to watch a play, only instead of there being a few people talking, there are a lot more people singing at very high volumes in an effort to be heard over the 50 or so folk sitting in front of them, inconveniently playing instruments incredibly loudly. Frankly, I don't know why they let them in.

But why do they sing?

Well, partly because long, loud, sustained noises are excellent at conveying emotion. That's why, when you stub your toe, you shout 'Aaaaaaaaaargh!' at the top of your voice. Mostly, though, it's because there's something about putting stories to really great music that makes them so much more powerful and affecting. Like that song about the baby shark. (If you don't know it, lucky you.)

So it's a bit like a musical, then?

It is, except in opera there's often no talking. They even sing the dialogue between the songs. I think they must get paid per note or something. Also, unlike in musicals, opera singers don't usually use microphones; what you hear is just what they can do with their lungs and larynx. It's either incredibly impressive or entirely terrifying, depending on how close you're sitting.

Is … is that a Viking?

What? Where? Ach! Yes, it is. Shoo! Shoo! I don't know where they come from. It's like a *How to Train Your Dragon* convention in here some days. I've had the council round but they say there's nothing they can do. Sorry. Go on.

Who are the singers?

Highly trained artistes who like to wear scarves and complain about air-conditioning. There are four main types. Sopranos, who have the highest voices and play the heroines. They also get the biggest bunch of flowers at the end, or there's trouble. Mezzo-sopranos, who have lower voices and often play men. In the old days male castratos would usually have played these roles, but that no longer happens for legal reasons. Tenors, men with higher voices who play the heroes and are a bit resentful about the sopranos getting the biggest bunch of flowers. And basses, who have the lowest voices and often play the baddies. I don't know why but for some reason we're supposed to associate low voices with evil, which does make you think differently about Santa.

What sort of stories do operas tell?

Oh, there's a tremendous variety. In *La bohème* a young poet called Rodolfo falls in love with a seamstress called Mimì who dies of consumption. In *Don Giovanni* the Don kills Donna Anna's dad and is dragged down to hell. In *Madam Butterfly* Cio-Cio-San is abandoned by her husband and kills herself. In *The Wreckers* Thirza and Mark are left to drown in the rising tide. In *Billy Budd* Billy is hanged for …

Hang on. Does everyone always die?

Well, not everyone. And not always. There are plenty of operatic comedies – Wagner's *The Mastersingers* is apparently one of them – but, if you are after a long and happy existence, you probably don't want to be an opera character. Very hard to get life insurance, I should think. Did you know that opera productions account for 73 per cent of all fake blood sales? I mean, that's a completely made-up statistic but no less impressive for that.

One last question. Do you know where I can buy a longboat?

Ugh. You're a Viking, aren't you? I should have guessed from the 'I ♥ Odin' T-shirt. Go on, get out! And take your axe with you! Actually, no. Leave that. We've got a production of Wagner's *Ring* coming up. Could come in handy. ●

Chris Addison is a comedian, actor, writer and director. He made his Royal Opera debut in the 2015–16 season as Smith in Chabrier's *L'étoile*.

Dido and Aeneas
PROM 7 • 19 JULY

The Wreckers
PROM 13 • 24 JULY

Il tabarro
PROM 19 • 30 JULY

See also Glass Handel (3 September)

Inform – Educate –
Entertain

As cult indie/electro-pop foursome PSB returns to the Proms, HELEN BROWN discovers the group's plans to delve into the BBC's audio archives for its new commission in the BBC's centenary year

I t's easy to forget just how powerful and strange the radio would have seemed to people when the BBC first began broadcasting in 1922,' says J. Willgoose, Esq. 'It would have felt like magic – a paradigm shift in the technology that would give people the opportunity to hear things they'd never have heard otherwise. The launch of BBC radio had the power to bind people together across the country in a way that had never happened before.'

So the shy frontman of gloriously geeky indie rock band Public Service Broadcasting has been 'amazed and daunted' by the prospect of writing new music to celebrate 100 years of the BBC.

Willgoose – not his real name – grew up in Tooting and attended a few Proms with his family. 'I'm not a traditional Prommer,' he says, 'but it's always been the most accessible way to hear classical music, hasn't it? It's one of the beacons of what the BBC does. If the Corporation stopped tomorrow, nobody else would step in and take over, would they?'

Always finding music the most direct way to distil the fizzy broth of his ideas, Willgoose slogged away as a guitarist in indie bands on the pub circuit through most of his twenties before founding PSB. The band began as a solo project with Willgoose first unveiling his blend

◀ Recapturing the past for the future: Public Service Broadcasting (*left to right*: JF Abraham, Mr B, J. Willgoose, Esq. and Wrigglesworth)

of electronic rock and visuals in Tooting before teaming up with geography teacher 'Wrigglesworth' (drums, piano) and shipping it up to the Edinburgh Fringe in 2010. Tickled to hear the British Film Institute had released some vintage recordings, he decided to drop some samples into the sound of the band's debut album, *Inform – Educate – Entertain* (2013): a title referencing the BBC's mission statement.

The album's propulsive theme was pioneering invention. Sampled audio clips focus on the first successful British expedition up Mount Everest in 1953, the development of the Spitfire fighter plane and the invention of colour television. It also included a sample of Marie Slocombe speaking about her work in the BBC's back offices. Born in 1912, Slocombe was a secretary employed to sort out dusty, heavy metal discs she found in the Corporation's archives. Her service included saving recordings by Winston Churchill, H. G. Wells and Edward VIII's 1936 abdication speech in which he confessed to the nation: 'I have found it impossible to carry the heavy burden of responsibility and to discharge my duties as King as I would wish to do without the help and support of the woman I love.' Though the BBC had been told not to keep a record of the seismic broadcast, Slocombe filed it for posterity. 'We kept on saying,' she recalled, 'this is for the listener of the future.'

Cutting through the synths, guitar, saxophone and determined motorik beats of PSB's debut album, you can

hear Slocombe explaining in crisp, crunchy RP: 'I'm not going to play you records by eminent people – you'll remember those – but I've chosen a few, from the many hundreds we are making. They deal with peak moments of intense personal experience. And I think together they say something about the spirit of our own time. Something that will still be worth saying 100 years hence.'

> 66 I would like to try and transport the audience back to a time when radio felt like transformative sorcery, beaming into people's homes across the country. 99

Since then, the corduroy-clad PSB unit has swelled to become a quartet with the admission of multi-instrumentalist 'JF Abraham' and 'Mr B' the 'visuals maestro'. They've burrowed deep into the world's sound archives to find samples exploring the Cold War and the quest to leave the Earth's orbit on *The Race for Space* (2015, the basis of their Proms debut in 2019) and brought in a choir to help interrogate the rise and fall of the Welsh coal-mining industry on *Every Valley* (2018). After relocating to Berlin for nine months, they made a love letter to the history and myths of the German capital: *Bright Magic* (2021) saw the band paying tribute to artists as diverse as David Bowie and Marlene Dietrich, while recording the fizzing of streetlights and the explosive tinkling of Willgoose smashing vintage light bulbs.

Band-leader and self-confessed 'corduroy-infected knob-twiddler' J. Willgoose, Esq., performing at Public Service Broadcasting's Proms debut in 2019 with an expanded version of the group's Moon-landing-inspired album *The Race for Space*

Willgoose says this new BBC piece 'won't be a chronological history of the BBC and it's not my job to bang the drum for the Corporation. They can do that much better themselves. I would like to try and transport the audience back to a time when radio felt like transformative sorcery, beaming into people's homes across the country.'

He says he'll enjoy ferreting around in the BBC archives for a sense of the British mood in the early 1920s, as the population recovered from the trauma of the Great War. Memorials rose along with the radio masts. King George V was on the throne and seeking to make the royal family more approachable to the British people. The 1921 Education Act raised the school leaving age to 14. Women over 30 were voting for the first time and Marie Stopes opened the first birth control clinic. Economically, the decade began with a boom and ended on bust.

When it comes to samples from the period, Willgoose is committed to 'avoiding the more obvious stuff. Our work has always been most effective when we've been exploring topics that people feel they know very well from different angles. When we did the moon landings on the album *The Race for Space* we didn't go for the 'One small step for man ...'-type business. We looked at the story from the perspective of Mission Control, examining the excitement of the technological narrative.'

He's interested in the narratives of the BBC's founding fathers: Lord Reith, Arthur Burrows and Cecil Lewis. 'I'll be asking: what did they hope the BBC would be? What function did they see it fulfilling? And I'll be drawing comparisons with where we are now and seeing if the organisation achieved their goals.'

Musically, Willgoose has been listening to 'Romantic, classical music' and Beatrice Harrison's 1924 cello duets with a nightingale in preparation for working with the BBC Symphony Orchestra. 'I'm not going to write an Elgar concerto,' he laughs. 'But, although we've arranged our existing songs for small orchestras before, we've never had the opportunity to write for and play with a symphony orchestra, so I want to really engage with them. I don't want to transplant lines from guitar to violin. I want to take full advantage of the breadth of emotional expression and power that you get with an orchestra of that size.'

PSB are thrilled to be returning to the Royal Albert Hall. Although Willgoose notes that in summer the venue can get a little warm for a guy who performs in a bow tie, he loves the way the building 'wraps its walls around you. Being on stage there is like being on a carousel – you can almost feel it turning, turning, turning ... It's an out-of-body experience.' ●

Helen Brown is Chief Pop Critic for the *Independent*, and has interviewed figures including Juliet Stevenson, Timothy Dalton and Julia Stone. She also writes for the *Telegraph* and the *Financial Times*.

**Public Service Broadcasting
This New Noise**
PROM 58 • 30 AUGUST

a star reborn

**THEATRE ROYAL
DRURY LANE**

FOOD, DRINK & DRAMA

OPEN ALL DAY, EVERY DAY
NO TICKET REQUIRED, BALLGOWNS OPTIONAL
MORE AT THELANE.CO.UK

Open *Score* Policy

Culminating in a unique Proms collaboration, BBC Open Music offers personalised training and development for 30 creatives from across the UK. **GEORGIA MANN**, a mentor on the scheme, speaks to some of those involved, and gets a taster of what we can expect from them this summer

We need to open the doors. Bring new people in. Listen and be bold,' says Jessica Isaacs, Head of Production at BBC Radio 3 and co-founder of a groundbreaking new training and development scheme, BBC Open Music, which brings a Prom unlike anything you'll have experienced before to the 2022 season. The aim is to draw new voices and perspectives to BBC Radio and Music – not just talk about doing so. Thirty creative people from across the UK have been selected for the scheme. Many of them have no past experience of the BBC Proms and most have never been to the Royal Albert Hall. The year-long programme connects the trainees with the world of BBC Radio and Music. They'll work closely with the BBC Concert Orchestra and Proms, receiving training on everything from pitching ideas to producing live radio – as well as one-on-one mentoring. Then they'll be handed the keys to the castle, collaborating with BBC teams to develop, produce and promote the first Open Music Prom – which you can experience on 1 September.

As well as being a Radio 3 presenter, I'm part of the team of Open Music mentors. There's one for each person on the scheme, and we come from all corners of BBC Radio and Music: from

◀ Class of 2022: BBC Open Music trainees in front of the Royal Albert Hall on their induction day last September

sound engineers to event producers, presenters to musicians. I jumped at the chance to become a mentor because I remember just how distant the goal of radio presenting felt when I was starting out, and I'm someone who came up the BBC ranks via local radio. The BBC can feel like an impenetrable place and making it behind one of those hallowed microphones can seem painfully unachievable. My mentee is 22-year-old Joseph Zubier, a classically trained singer from Northern Ireland. For Joseph, the opportunity to be part of the Proms is really something special: 'I can't understate the importance of the BBC Proms in the classical music world; its easily among the most influential festivals in the calendar. For me, the main highlight of Open Music is that our team has been given the opportunity to lead the conversation around classical music, steering it in a way that we think will benefit the widest range of people. We hope to reach audiences that have never even heard of the Proms, let alone been to one. And we're going to try to do this while also appealing to our established audiences. It's a real honour, and we're all humbled by it.'

We know that classical music needs to do more to ensure that its orchestras and choirs, as well as its audiences, are representative of everyone living in the UK. In February 2020 Claire Mera-Nelson, Director of Music at Arts Council England, said: 'The workforce of our orchestras and ensembles is not fully reflective of the diverse society in

which we live. The culture, repertoire, presentation and audiences of classical music all appear to introduce barriers to participation.' Bill Chandler is Director of the BBC Concert Orchestra, which will be working with the Open Music team: 'This orchestra is used to working in genre-busting mediums, and is perfectly placed to deliver what we hope will be a groundbreaking Proms experience. Orchestral music has historically focused on the core repertoire from its European origins but we are beginning to widen our thinking and programming. It is essential that we create ways to connect with more people, new people and communities that haven't had easy access to the BBC performing groups.'

> ❝ The range of ideas presented has been quite extraordinary; not one of the six pitches was remotely the same as any another … none was like anything I've ever seen at the Proms before. ❞

BBC Radio 6 Music presenter Mary Anne Hobbs is co-founder of BBC Open Music. She masterminded a 2015 Prom featuring American ambient music duo A Winged Victory For The Sullen, pianist Nils Frahm and dancers from Company Wayne McGregor – so she knows a thing or two about taking the Proms into new territory. 'A labour of great love for all of

The 30 BBC Open Music trainees; together they are working on a 'groundbreaking' new Prom that they hope 'will draw a new generation into the Royal Albert Hall'

Ricardo Burt, is currently studying for a Broadcasting diploma: 'As someone who rarely listened to classical music, I wanted to learn more about the genre. I also felt I could provide a vital perspective, as someone who always found it hard to engage with it.' What does Ricardo make of the Proms? 'Originally I thought it was old-fashioned and not very experimental. However, being able to watch an orchestra rehearse before a performance was an eye-opening experience. I saw first-hand the experimentation, the conductor adapting the sound and style.' Keeley Ray says: 'As a self-taught, Northern music producer, the Proms has always been something that seemed inaccessible to a person like me. It should be a place for all – no matter your age, gender, where you're from or how you identify. The Open Music Prom will be a statement of that.'

There's clearly no lack of resolve among this group. But there's the small matter of planning. How did this super-diverse cohort channel their ideas? 'We met for the first time at an induction, on a very hot September day during the 2021 Proms season,' says Jessica Isaacs. 'We gave the trainees an insight into the BBC and the Proms. Then in December we ran two pitch development days. Split into six teams, they were challenged to think about the target audience, what the experience feels like for Prommers in the Hall or listening on air, the presentation, marketing, social media campaign and much more. By the end of the second day each team had pitched their ideas, which we then put to a vote.'

us involved' is how Hobbs describes the scheme. 'The group we are working with is wildly creative, curious, ambitious and free-thinking. The aim of the project is to re-imagine what a Prom can be in the BBC's centenary year.'

So who are these 30 wildly creative people? Some are musicians: Keeley Ray is a Liverpool-based composer of electronic music; Aano Sodipe is a composer who takes inspiration from her parents' Yoruba heritage. There's also Rebecca Oberg, a Swedish theatre-maker and film-maker with a focus on queer work, and Leo Geyer, founder of Constella OperaBallet. Another mentee, 19-year-old

I asked my mentee, Joseph, how it felt to be part of this Prom pitching process. I've presented and produced plenty of Proms and, I have to admit, the thought of starting out with a blank sheet of paper makes my pulse-rate accelerate somewhat. Joseph says: 'When I tell you that these sessions have been fruitful, that's the understatement of the year! The range of ideas presented has been quite extraordinary; not one of the six pitches was remotely the same as any other ... none was like anything I've ever seen at the Proms before – in the best possible way!' Some of the suggestions included having an 'exploded' orchestra spaced throughout the Hall, handing programming control over to the audience via a voting app and creating a multi-sensory environment.

As the Proms Festival Guide goes to press, the Open Music Prom is still in the very early stages of development. 'I think this Prom will draw a new generation into the Royal Albert Hall, people who may never have imagined that they'd be hanging out at a Prom in this life or the next,' says Mary Anne Hobbs. Keeley Ray emphasises the audience focus we can expect from the Prom: 'I'm excited to bring new ideas and new patterns to the stage, to bring the audience on a journey they've never experienced before. The world doesn't look like it did 100 years ago – and our Prom will reflect that. It will be an electrifying show that uses contemporary instrumentation and technology to present the stories of our time.' Joseph Zubier is aware that the stakes are high. 'There's definitely an element of risk ... Some might say: "What if people don't come? What if people think it's too 'out there'?" But experimenting with innovative and inclusive approaches to concerts is the only way classical music is going to appeal to future audiences and keep up with a fast-changing world. We have to ask ourselves: "Why would someone come to a concert when they can listen to music for free on Spotify or YouTube?" It's our job as creatives to provide an experience for audiences that they can't get anywhere else and, to do that, we have to take risks and try new things.'

It's the willingness of those involved in the scheme to try something new that appeals to me. The language and jargon around 'diversity' can often seem so empty, but here we have a real chance to step outside the conventions of concert programming and hear from people whose backgrounds don't match the traditional profile of a music-industry player. I asked Jessica Isaacs what had most surprised her about the Open Music endeavour so far: 'The spirit that seems to bind the 30 trainees together. None of them knew each other beforehand and they seemed to gel so quickly. They come with no preconceptions and are open to everything. The name of our scheme, Open Music, seems just right for them!' ●

Georgia Mann presents Radio 3's BBC Radio 3's Essential Classics.

BBC Open Music Prom

PROM 60 • 1 SEPTEMBER

Young Voices at the Proms

BBC Young Composer 2022

BBC Young Composer continues to discover, nurture and platform young talent aged 12–18 who create their own music. Join the BBC Concert Orchestra at Battersea Arts Centre on Saturday 30 July to hear the premieres of works by 2021 competition winners Chelsea Becker, Isaac Bristow, Maddy Chassar-Hesketh, Will Everitt, Theo Kendall and Jenna Stewart, as well as a piece by 2019 winner Daniel Liu. See page 124 for details.

If you are a musician aged 12–18 interested in creating your own music, visit bbc.co.uk/youngcomposer to find out more about online activities and events.

Zac Pile

❝ BBC Young Composer offers you the rare luxury of having the time to try stuff in a safe place.

Zac Pile, a winner in the Lower Junior category of BBC Young Composer 2020

Proms at Sage Gateshead

In partnership with Sage Gateshead, the BBC Proms will work with young singers aged 16–30 to form a new large-scale youth choir for the North-East, Voices of the River's Edge. You can hear them perform with chamber-folk collective Spell Songs on Saturday 23 July as part of Proms at Sage Gateshead. See page 121 for details.

◀ Piercing vision: the Philips Pavilion, designed by architect-turned-composer Iannis Xenakis for the Brussels World's Fair, 1958; its form is based on a cluster of nine hyperbolic paraboloids

Sound *by Design*

Born 100 years ago, Iannis Xenakis was one of the giants of 20th-century music, who uniquely harnessed mathematical principles to create sonic worlds of breathtakingly imaginative abstraction, says composer JULIAN ANDERSON

In 1958, with the Second World War over a decade past, the Brussels World's Fair celebrated the latest achievements in technology and the arts. Visitors were struck by a strangely shaped, asymmetrically swooping edifice jutting out at sharp angles – the Philips Pavilion – designed, though it looked quite unlike his other buildings, by the most famous living architect, Le Corbusier. Except that it wasn't: in reality it was the work of his Greek assistant, Iannis Xenakis, at that time becoming known as a composer. Visitors to the Pavilion, inside which Le Corbusier mounted a multimedia show of dubious taste ('showing evolution from the ape to Le Corbusier,' quipped one of Philips's directors), would probably not have been much mollified by being told that the building's design was modelled from the shape of the gliding swoops drawn in the score of Xenakis's recent orchestral work *Metastaseis* (1953–4) in the form of hyperbolic paraboloids.

For a man who had lost part of his face in the aftermath of the Second World War, and who barely 11 years previously had fled to Paris illegally on a fake passport, seeing his first major building unveiled must have seemed like an apotheosis, even if his famous boss initially took all the credit. Xenakis had lost his mother at the age of 5 and spent an unhappy period at a British-style boarding school. He had almost matriculated from Athens University with an engineering degree by the start of the war – during which he was nearly killed several times over. But these traumatic experiences had also been instructive. Leading anti-Nazi demonstrations in the centre of Athens, Xenakis noticed how the rhythmically chanted slogans he initiated were gradually transformed into chaos as the crowd encountered the enemy in the central square. Years later, he repeatedly and memorably recreated those transformations from order to disorder in his music.

Xenakis was a natural rebel. An outsider at school (despite his prowess at sports), he took nothing for granted. Initially attracted to Communism, he was quickly disillusioned by its ghastly reality. From then on he refused all dogmas and looked at things his own way. When he arrived in Paris in 1947, aside from earning his living working for Le Corbusier, he took lessons from the most celebrated French composer of the time, Olivier Messiaen. Aware that by Paris Conservatoire standards his own musical technique was virtually nil, he bravely asked Messiaen if he should start from scratch to learn all the basics – harmony, counterpoint, and so on. To his surprise, Messiaen said no: Xenakis should use his knowledge of maths, engineering and architecture in his compositions. This, Messiaen assured him, would enable him to build a technique of his own.

And that, for the next 50 years, is precisely what Xenakis did. Initially mocked for his lack of musical training by such Serialist hotheads as Pierre Boulez (who never did appreciate his music), with great patience and a strong imagination Xenakis carefully rethought every element of music. The sonic results have shocked audiences ever since – as one commentator put it, 'One does not

Xenakis in 1983: despite his fascination with mathematical principles, he believed that music's aim was 'to draw towards a total exaltation in which the individual mingles, losing their consciousness in a truth immediate, rare, enormous and perfect'

go to a Xenakis premiere to have one's ears soothed.' Indeed not. The visceral energy of a piece like *Eonta* (1963–4) for piano and brass can be almost too much to take. Passages of eerie void stand beside eruptions of volcanic fury. 'Is your music deliberately violent?' a British interviewer once asked him. 'Maybe yes, maybe no,' the composer equivocated. Nevertheless, increasing exposure

brought not only critical applause but growing appreciation from the public – though often not the conventional concert public. The rawness of his expression got through to alternative rock crowds uninterested in Beethoven, and he became a cult figure, with even The Beatles showing his influence in the dense string glissandos near the end of 'A Day in the Life' from *Sgt. Pepper's Lonely Hearts Club Band* (producer George Martin's doing, perhaps). His music is still popular on the rock circuit, along with that of his friend Edgard Varèse (whose *Poème électronique* was composed especially to be heard in the Philips Pavilion) and his contemporaries Karlheinz Stockhausen and Luigi Nono – alternative heroes whose daring and boldness remain lodestars for anyone wishing to push boundaries.

British concert audiences have generally responded with startled gratitude and, during his lifetime, were charmed by Xenakis's modest demeanour and gentle humour. Neither of these qualities found their way into his music, but it's not emotionally neutral – far from it. The anguished cries of *Nuits* (1967–8) for 12 voices, dedicated to political prisoners in his native Greece and elsewhere, or the uniquely searing howls of *Aïs* (1980) for amplified baritone and orchestra (both of which have previously featured at the Proms) speak of a mind deeply concerned with the human condition. The ancient Greek texts of *Aïs*, from Homer and Sappho, include a lament for a dead mother: given that Xenakis lost his own mother so young, this is certainly not coincidental. *Jonchaies*, featured at this year's Proms, is perhaps his masterpiece. Its 16 minutes unfold in a single, continuously evolving sonic avalanche, testing the strengths of both players and audience alike. Xenakis was a great fan of wild-water kayaking, especially in dangerous weather, and by the end of *Jonchaies* you may well feel as though you're lucky to have survived. The rewards are rich, however: an experience of overwhelming excitement, exhilaration and terrifying beauty unique in the orchestral literature.

When his health failed him, with characteristic decisiveness Xenakis composed *O-Mega* (1997), named after the final letter of the Greek alphabet, for the percussionist Evelyn Glennie, and laid down his pen. His centenary gives us all the chance to explore an output as varied as it is unusual, the product of one of the most cultivated yet savagely powerful imaginations music has given us. ●

Julian Anderson was Professor of Composition at Harvard University (2004–7) and is currently Composer in Residence and Professor of Composition at the Guildhall School of Music & Drama. His BBC-commissioned Symphony No. 2, 'Prague Panoramas', will receive its UK premiere in Prom 26 (5 August).

Allegro molto; Akea; Ittidra;
À r. (Hommage à Ravel)
PROMS AT BELFAST • 18 JULY

Jonchaies
PROM 20 • 31 JULY

O-Mega
PROM 22 • 2 AUGUST

An Unexplained Phenomenon

Composer Betsy Jolas *(see Prom 66)* recalls her friendship with Iannis Xenakis

I believe I first met Iannis Xenakis in 1954, in Paris. I was then a student at the Conservatoire in the class of Darius Milhaud, and we were asked to take a session at Pierre Schaeffer's experimental GRM (Groupe de Recherches Musicales) studios. Xenakis already seemed established there: he had his own studio and didn't have to follow the regular classes.

We soon began to get on quite well and we would often go out for drinks with other students. This was when Pierre Boulez was establishing his Domaine Musical concert series. At the same time, people were becoming interested in György Ligeti and Krzysztof Penderecki as well as Xenakis, though his approach was very different.

Boulez recognised Xenakis's rising renown and included him in one of the Domaine concerts. And so the first piece of his that I heard live was at the Domaine Musical: it was *Eonta*, for piano and brass quintet. I remember attending in 1964 the rehearsal for the premiere of that piece, which Boulez was conducting. It starts with a wild piano solo of a little over one minute. I wondered for a while why Xenakis had decided to write out the precise pitches rather than leave them free because it seemed at the time that this solo was practically unplayable. The pianist, Yuji Takahashi, was faking it pretty well but Boulez couldn't follow and missed the entrance of the quintet. He was pretty mad about that!

I was anxious to learn how Xenakis's mind worked, so I bought his book, *Musiques formelles* ('Formalised Music') but, of course, I had trouble understanding what he was talking about since he wrote as an architect and an engineer, not as a musician. I realise today that I never actually followed his thinking, which was very different from mine. This did not prevent us from being good friends throughout his life.

We got to know each other even better through a trip to Bali in 1972 with the composer Takemitsu and others. We were privileged to hear many different gamelans (traditional Indonesian ensembles) and Xenakis would record everything. To us Europeans it seemed there was music at every corner: there was always some celebration going on that required music. One of the first pieces that came out of this trip was Xenakis's beautiful *Jonchaies*, which was obviously influenced by some of the haunting tunes we heard in Bali.

Eventually I gave up trying to understand how Xenakis's mind worked but I was very interested in the way he sometimes asked for unusual playing techniques that had never been used before. But, as the years went by, the impossible became possible.

It's still an unexplained mystery to me that, although Xenakis did not think musically the way we did, he could move us with his music so beautifully. So we should no longer bother about 'how' to hear his music. We should just listen!

Master *and* *Student*

For over six decades, Amjad Ali Khan has toured internationally as one of India's foremost exponents of the sarod. As he returns to the Proms, SANGEETA DATTA outlines his standing in the Indian classical music world and his place within a distinguished, and continuing, family line of musicians

A father figure in today's sarod world, Amjad Ali Khan is equally at ease playing for an audience of thousands as he is taking a reflective walk alone. Likewise, his glamorous stage presence contrasts with his introspective musical meditation in practice at his instrument. His dexterous movements across the sarod strings have reached millions through live concerts and recordings. With his mellifluous voice he sings song-patterns before he plays them. I have childhood memories of midnight magic as he struck up the late-night *Raga Darbari* and of rose-hued dawns breaking as he played *Raga Lalit* to conclude all-night classical concerts and music festivals.

Khan is the sixth-generation sarod player in the ancient Bangash family. He trained under his father, the respected sarod player Haafiz Ali Khan, who was a musician at the royal court of Gwalior until India gained independence in 1947. Haafiz Ali gave his youngest son, Amjad Ali, his debut concert at the age of 6, presenting him to the elite audience. As Indian classical music began to reach a global audience in the 1960s, Amjad Ali became known as the 'Prince of Sarod'.

Amjad Ali Khan's ancestors moulded the present-day sarod from its beginnings in the form of the Afghan rabab, a plucked, lute-like folk instrument that travelled

◄ Glamorous yet introspective: Amjad Ali Khan performing at Virginia Beach, Virginia, in 2019

from Central Asia with the foot soldiers playing marching tunes in the Mughal armies. During the 18th century, Amjad's ancestor, Mohammad Hashmi Khan, a musician and horsetrader, brought the Afghan rabab to India and settled in the royal court of Rewa in Madhya Pradesh. Mohammad's grandson, Ghulam Ali Khan Bangash (Amjad Ali's great-grandfather), lived in the royal court of Gwalior. In his hands the rabab evolved into the sarod, one of the central instruments in Indian classical music. Structurally, the rabab's skin was replaced by a long metal fingerboard, and the catgut strings changed to sophisticated metal strings. As a result, the staccato sound was transformed into a more lyrical, vocal quality. The technique of this school, or *gharana*, of pressing down on the metal strings with the fingernails of the left hand, produced a clear sound and allowed long slides between the melody notes, which hold great emotional resonance.

Both Ghulam Ali Khan and his grandson Haafiz Ali Khan received training from the family of the legendary singer Miyan Tansen in Gwalior, where they settled. Tansen was court musician in the Mughal court of Emperor Akbar and there are innumerable stories about this magical singer and his control over Indian ragas. The Bangash family musicians combined their sarod style (*Bangash gharana*) with the tradition of instrumental music in the Tansen style (*Seniya gharana*).

Amjad Ali Khan won over audiences at home and overseas. Awards and recognition flowed in, including

the Crystal Award from the World Economic Forum, UNICEF's National Ambassadorship and the Fukuoka Grand Prize. For him the sarod is a singing instrument, very close to the human voice, and he wishes to express every human expression through the instrument. Each day he sings as much as he plays during his *riyaz* (practice).

The sarod is the Bangash family instrument and Amjad Ali's sons Amaan and Ayaan are both distinguished players in their own right, who often perform with their father. They represent the seventh generation of this great family legacy. Moving with the times, they have played fusion music and hosted television shows. Their father is proud that their new work is rooted in the classical tradition, as they navigate a path between continuity and change, tradition and innovation. And there are glimpses of the eighth generation of Bangash musicians, as Ayaan's twin sons pick up their baby-sized sarods and practise with their grandfather. Fittingly, Amjad Ali Khan's ancestral home in Gwalior has been turned into the Sarod Ghar, or House of Sarod, a museum, resource for study and platform for young players.

Soft-spoken and introverted, with his silken grey hair, Amjad Ali Khan (or 'Khansahib', as I call him) displays a Sufi-like disposition. He performed a 'Raga for Peace' at the 2014 Nobel Peace Prize Concert in Oslo (he is passionate about bringing peace through music) and appeared with the Refugee Orchestra Project at the 2018 United Nations Day

Concert. He has also graced the stages of New York's Carnegie Hall, Washington DC's Kennedy Center and the Sydney Opera House. But, as well as performing traditional ragas or melodies, he has also created new music: he has composed many new ragas and his first sarod concerto, *Samaagam*, has been performed internationally. He has always sought out new conversations through his music, whether collaborating with musicians in Carnatic (South Indian) or Bengali music, or with Girija Devi, the queen of the vocal style of *thumri*, or creating new work with young students and artists in residencies at Stanford and New Mexico universities. His diverse musical range also embraces songs by the poet and composer Rabindranath Tagore and folk songs of Assam and Bengal. Last year he and his sons recorded an EP with American rock guitarist Joe Walsh.

A practising Muslim, Amjad Ali is married to a Hindu, Subhalakshmi, to whom he has dedicated a raga. At a time of religious tensions in India, Khansahib's words reflect his all-embracing world-view as well as an epiphanic vision of music: 'Music has no religion, it transcends barriers. I feel I connect to every human soul with my instrument. My music connects me with God: sublime sound is God.' ●

Writer/director, film-maker and cultural commentator Sangeeta Datta has known Amjad Ali Khan for many years. Her films include the full-length *Life Goes On*, as well as documentaries and shorts. She runs Baithak UK, which promotes South Indian arts in the UK.

Amjad Ali Khan, Amaan Ali Bangash and Ayaan Ali Bangash
PROM 45 • 21 AUGUST, 11.30am

Body and Soul

The story of the sarod, one of the key instruments of North Indian classical music

The sarod is as popular and predominant in North Indian classical music as the sitar. But, compared to the sitar, it produces a sound that is somewhat weightier, deeper and more resonant, enabling its players to unfold delicate tonal qualities and explore some of the finest nuances of Indian classical music. In the Persian language, the word 'sarod' means 'beautiful melody'.

A plucked string instrument, the sarod is shorter than the sitar and rests in the performer's lap. In addition to the main resonating chamber at the bottom, made of teak and covered with goatskin, some instruments have a smaller additional chamber at the top end, made of metal. The instrument itself is made of a single block of wood, consisting of a hollow, circular belly extending into a tapering neck that arches back slightly to end in a peg box. The front of the belly is covered by parchment while the fingerboard, across which the metal strings are tightly placed, is made of highly polished metal.

The specific design of the sarod depends very much on the *gharana* (or musical family-style) of the exponent who is playing it. There are two main techniques of sarod playing: one in which the strings are pressed (or stopped) by the fingertips of the left hand and the other in which the strings are stopped by the fingernails. It's the second method (the one adopted by Amjad Ali Khan) that is said to produce a very clear, ringing sound but is considered very difficult to execute.

The conventional sarod can have 19 to 25 strings, of which four or five are used for playing the melody. There are usually one or two drone strings, plus two high-pitched drone strings (known as *chikari*) for rhythmic articulation, as well as anything from nine to 11 sympathetic strings that vibrate freely. The strings are played by being plucked with a plectrum made out of a piece of coconut shell.

Although more than one hereditary Indian music family has claimed to have invented the instrument, it is generally agreed that the sarod is a descendant of the Afghan rabab and that an Afghan ancestor of Amjad Ali Khan introduced the instrument to India in the mid-18th century. But there is also some speculation that the sarod could have evolved from the ancient Middle Eastern lute known as the oud. Whether its origins lie in Central Asia or in the Middle East, the sarod is supremely suited to Indian classical music and, because it is unfretted, the facility to slide between notes (glissando or *meenh*) is greatly enhanced. But this very lack of frets, coupled with tight and tense strings, makes this one of the most difficult instruments to play, requiring not just wrist action but also considerable strength in the shoulder of the playing arm.

The sarod first became known internationally largely due to the concert appearances of the legendary Ali Akbar Khan; he had trained under his father Allauddin Khan, who also simultaneously trained Ravi Shankar on sitar. In turn, Allauddin Khan was taught by Wazir Khan, the teacher also of Amjad Ali Khan's father, Haafiz Ali Khan.

Jameela Siddiqi is an award-winning broadcaster, novelist, journalist and lecturer in the history and theory of Indian classical music.

Music and more

Continue your musical experience
at the Royal College of Music,
opposite the Royal Albert Hall,
with concerts, café, courtyard
and a beautiful new museum.

rcm.ac.uk/explore

ROYAL

COLLEGE

OF MUSIC

London

Mood *Music*

Ahead of a Proms season that features over 10 world premieres, three of this year's commissioned composers put their creative process under the microscope, exploring the themes and inspirations behind their latest work in the form of musical 'mood boards'.

Summer Lovin'
In 'Summer' the departing swarm gives way to a new Queen, represented in the music by percussion (including the harp's soundboard). She then sets to work repopulating the hive.

Sally Beamish

Hive *world premiere*
PROM 9 • 21 JULY

Born in London, Sally Beamish began her professional life as a viola player before moving to Scotland to pursue composition. The starting point for her music is often strongly personal, based on a relationship or event. Her harp concerto, *Hive*, is one such piece. It was written for the Welsh harpist Catrin Finch, whom Beamish heard in concert alongside the Colombian band Cimarrón in 2020.

What's the Buzz?
Based on an idea for a dance piece by playwright Peter Thomson, *Hive* explores the life of a beehive over four movements or 'seasons'.

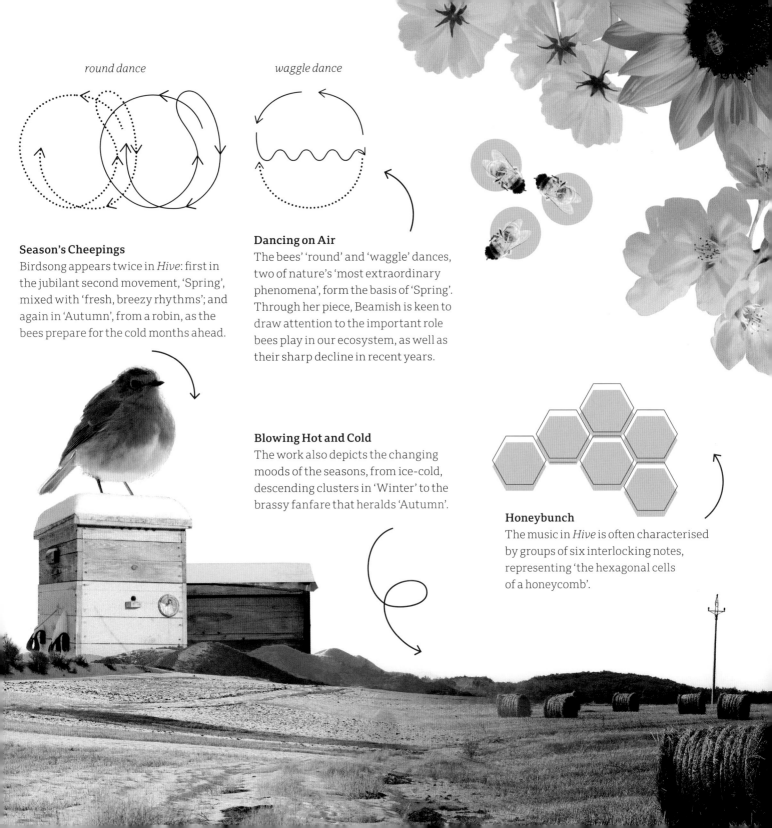

round dance

waggle dance

Season's Cheepings
Birdsong appears twice in *Hive*: first in the jubilant second movement, 'Spring', mixed with 'fresh, breezy rhythms'; and again in 'Autumn', from a robin, as the bees prepare for the cold months ahead.

Dancing on Air
The bees' 'round' and 'waggle' dances, two of nature's 'most extraordinary phenomena', form the basis of 'Spring'. Through her piece, Beamish is keen to draw attention to the important role bees play in our ecosystem, as well as their sharp decline in recent years.

Blowing Hot and Cold
The work also depicts the changing moods of the seasons, from ice-cold, descending clusters in 'Winter' to the brassy fanfare that heralds 'Autumn'.

Honeybunch
The music in *Hive* is often characterised by groups of six interlocking notes, representing 'the hexagonal cells of a honeycomb'.

Hildur Guðnadóttir

new work *world premiere*
PROM 8 • 20 JULY

Although born in Iceland, Hildur Guðnadóttir has been based in Berlin since the early 2000s. There she has built a formidable career as a composer and performer, working across experimental pop, the classical avant-garde, theatre, television and film. Her recent scores to Todd Phillips's *Joker* and the HBO series *Chernobyl* have brought her into mainstream consciousness, winning an Academy Award and a Grammy respectively, while past commissioners include the Iceland Symphony Orchestra, Royal Swedish Opera and London's Tate Modern. Guðnadóttir's compositions often have a specific idea or theme at their core, but in this new work – her first BBC Proms commission – she has drawn upon her eclectic mix of musical and non-musical experiences to create a tapestry of 'miniature, moving elements'.

Atomic Written
Guðnadóttir's process reminds her of a ytterbium cloud, in which many millions of atoms converge to form a vivid and cohesive whole. This is particularly evident in this piece.

Quiet City
Guðnadóttir's home city, Berlin, allows her the space and solitude required to create: 'It's such a slow and heavy city, and that helps me to hear my thoughts.'

Picture Perfect
When writing, Guðnadóttir often uses a visual aid 'to help focus my attention'. For this piece, she painted a triangle whose three sides represent 1) physical health, 2) mental health and 3) their joint necessity for her to 'function as a person'.

All the Small Things
Like many composers, Guðnadóttir draws inspiration from the world around her. But it's the small things that she tries to encapsulate in her work: 'Some can't see the wood for the trees, but I can't see the trees for the lichen on the bark.'

'The Paintings for the Temple'
For Guðnadóttir, art is a 'continuous process', with each work forming one part in a representative whole. Klint's 1906–15 *Temple* series, comprising 193 works, embodies this idea.

Secret Weapon
Decades ahead of her time, the Swedish abstractionist Hilma af Klint (1862–1944) has been a huge inspiration to Guðnadóttir, in part because she kept her paintings secret: 'She knew the world wasn't ready, and that reactions to her work would influence her own connection to it. She truly lived her art.'

Missy Mazzoli

Violin Concerto, 'Procession' *European premiere*
PROM 38 • 14 AUGUST

Born in a small town in Pennsylvania, Missy Mazzoli moved to New York in the 2000s, establishing herself with an upfront take on Minimalism: electric, but with deep historical references, often written for her own group, Victoire, in which she plays keyboards. Since then the scope of her compositions has expanded into orchestral music and opera, with commissions from the Chicago Symphony Orchestra – where she was Mead Composer in Residence – and the Metropolitan Opera, New York. Yet her 'apocalyptic imagination' – as *The New Yorker*'s Alex Ross called it – has remained a constant.

Written in five movements, or 'spells', Mazzoli's Violin Concerto draws inspiration from humanity's long history of spiritual healing. Charms, soothsayers and penitential processions all feature in a piece packed with medieval and macabre imagery. But, typical of Mazzoli's work, there's room for a little humour too.

By the Book
The fourth movement's title, 'Bone to Bone, Blood to Blood', is derived from the second 'Merseburg Charm', a *c*9th-century German spell for curing broken limbs.

Walking Wounded
'Procession in a Spiral', the first movement of the concerto, recreates a medieval penitential procession.

Band Aid
The concerto takes 'energetic' inspiration from Brooklyn-based experimental rock band Black Dice, which Mazzoli saw while composing her piece; their latest album, *Mod Prog Sic*, was released last year.

Animal Magic
Mazzoli's companion for much of the time she spent writing the concerto, Beulah the French Bulldog was an inescapable influence on her music.

Koh-Conspirator
Written for her longtime friend and collaborator Jennifer Koh, Mazzoli's concerto was conceived with the violinist's own musical personality in mind. (Koh will be performing the piece this summer at its Proms premiere.)

Follow the Leader
Mazzoli casts the soloist as a 'soothsayer, sorcerer, healer and Pied Piper-type character', who leads the orchestra through a sequence of five 'healing spells'.

Rock Music
Mazzoli wrote much of the concerto while in residence at Ingmar Bergman's estate on the Swedish island of Fårö, famed for its rocky beach formations.

Dancing with Death
The second movement pays homage to Vitus, the patron saint of dancing. Sydenham chorea – or 'Saint Vitus' Dance' – is a disease that causes involuntary muscle spasms; in the Middle Ages those afflicted would attend chapels of Saint Vitus in search of a cure.

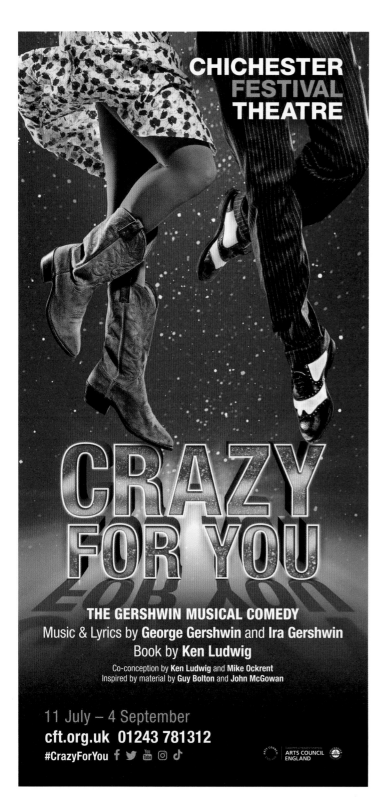

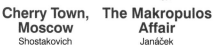

◀ Proms progression: 2015's 'Ibiza' Prom brought Radio 1 (and DJ Pete Tong) to the Proms for the first time — a typical marriage of artistic adventure and broadcasting capability in a season that also saw collaborations with Radios 1 Xtra, 2, 4 and 6 Music

The **Proms** *and the* **BBC**

In the year the BBC turns 100, former Proms Director NICHOLAS KENYON charts the history of a unique partnership, begun in 1927, that has shaped how music meets audiences in the world's largest classical music festival

Not all marriages are made in heaven. Partnerships between organisations, each with their own stories and their own values, are notoriously difficult to sustain over the long term. But the coming-together of the Henry Wood Promenade Concerts and the nascent British Broadcasting Company in the 1920s is the exception that proves the rule: it was an ideal marriage of aims and ambitions that has renewed itself constantly over the years into a new era of technology and distribution, establishing the BBC Proms as a world leader in making great music available to everyone.

The familiar narrative is that the BBC heroically stepped in to save the Proms in 1927 but the picture is more subtle than that. Who needed whom? From its origin exactly a century ago in 1922, the British Broadcasting Company needed music. Live music, alongside news, was

the staple diet of its programmes, and a constant supply of orchestral pieces from its regional centres was essential for its audiences. In line with John Reith's mission to 'inform, educate and entertain', the BBC began to take responsibility for promoting its own concerts, while sometimes relaying larger events such as opera from Covent Garden that it could not mount itself. Assailed by the music profession and promoters who believed that broadcasting would kill attendance at live events, the BBC showed that the evidence was exactly the opposite – an early enthusiast, the Organiser of Programmes C. A. Lewis, wrote ecstatically of the early impact of a broadcast of Mozart's *The Magic Flute* on opera attendances.

The Proms had developed since 1895 under the watchful eye of promoter Robert Newman and the galvanising presence of conductor Henry Wood into a concert series of great impact;

it used the Queen's Hall in central London with its stalls seats removed to create a standing arena and welcomed newly mobile audiences from the suburbs. Newman's aims were remarkably similar to John Reith's. As Wood recalled, 'He wanted the public to come to love great music. "I am going to … train the public by easy stages," he said. "Popular at first, gradually raising the standard until I have *created* a public for classical and modern music."' Wood had supported this aim and moved the early Proms programmes on from a diet dominated by arias and operatic medleys to major symphonies, concertos and what Wood called his 'novelties' – new music from the most adventurous sources on the Continent, from Debussy and Strauss (who fared well with audiences) to Schoenberg and Mahler (less so).

But the Proms was always financially fragile, dependent on private investment, and in 1926, with the death of Robert

FOR THE HONOUR OF LONDON.

Shade of Beethoven (Father of Modern Symphonic Music) to Sir Henry Wood. "THIS IS INDEED TRAGIC, BUT I CANNOT BELIEVE THAT THIS RICH CITY, ONCE SO GENEROUS TO ME, WILL FAIL TO FIND US A PERMANENT HOME."

LEFT – Adrian Boult conducting the BBC Symphony Orchestra at the Last Night of the Proms in 1947; part of the concert was televised using only two cameras, and was the first TV broadcast of an orchestral concert in the UK

RIGHT – The shade of Beethoven reassures Proms founder-conductor Henry Wood in a *Punch* cartoon (March 1927) that a new sponsor would be found for the Proms: the BBC took over the running of the festival that summer

Newman, the festival's then supporter, the music publisher Chappell under its sceptical managing director William Boosey announced it could no longer promote the season. Wood protested, 'We have done so much that I am sure we are going to do a great deal more.' The press was mobilised: a famous *Punch* cartoon shows the ghost of Beethoven appearing to Wood with the caption: FOR THE HONOUR OF LONDON: Shade of Beethoven (Father of Modern Symphonic Music) to Sir Henry Wood: 'This is indeed tragic, but I cannot believe that this rich city, once so generous to me, will fail to find us a permanent home.'

Here then for the BBC was both a major opportunity and a responsibility – to acquire a prestigious concert series

whose artistic ambitions matched its own educative intent and, through broadcasting, to make it available to all listeners. The complex turmoil of the negotiations with Wood have been preserved in all their argumentative detail, with Wood worried that the BBC might interfere with his single-handed choice of players and his grasp of the repertoire. In the end an agreement was reached just in time for the 1927 Proms season to be planned with Wood's indefatigable concerts organiser, W. W. Thompson, in just a few breathless weeks.

The process of collaboration between the BBC (it became established as the Corporation in that same year, 1927) and the Proms was not always totally smooth – hardly surprising given the forcefulness of Henry Wood's personality and the public service rigour of the BBC mandarins. But it soon became clear that what broadcasting created for the Proms was – and still is – something extraordinary and indeed precious. Through being relayed to a wider public than those who could attend, the season took its place alongside sporting, royal and ceremonial occasions as one of the landmarks of British national life. The media historian Paddy Scannell has written that these events 'became, and have remained, punctual moments in a shared national life. Broadcasting created, in effect, a new calendar of national events.' There may no longer be quite so secure a cultural consensus around these occasions, but one need look no further for an explanation of why events at the Proms, and especially its Last Night, take on a significance far beyond that of a concert.

From an initial BBC scepticism that Wood could sustain his leadership of the Proms through the 1930s, there came an understanding of just how strongly the audience related to the season through his advocacy and personality. While Adrian Boult and a succession of major guest conductors led the BBC Symphony Orchestra, formed in 1930, to great heights in its winter season, the Proms flourished under Wood through to his death in 1944. 'With the whole-hearted support of the wonderful medium of broadcasting,' said Wood, 'I feel that I am at last on the threshold of realising my lifelong ambition of truly democratising the message of music.' That democratising message

has remained constant across the years, thanks both to broadcasting and to best-value ticket prices in the hall, especially for the standing places.

There was one interruption in the continuing relationship between the Proms and the BBC. When war broke out in 1939, the BBC Symphony Orchestra was moved to Bristol and the BBC could not support a Proms season in London. Wood arranged a substitute season, which lasted only four weeks, and in May 1941 the BBC's fears of disruption in London were sadly justified when the Queen's Hall, home of the Proms since its inception, was blitzed. However, this setback proved an opportunity for the joint enterprise. In 1941 the Proms moved to the Royal Albert Hall, and in 1942 the BBC took back the promotion of the season.

The post-war years were a time of huge growth in all cultural activities: new festivals were founded, the BBC's Third Programme began, and the Proms flourished with larger audiences than ever. The orchestral duties were now shared between several orchestras, allowing for more rehearsal time and better preparation, and the broadcasts were shared between the BBC's new radio networks – not just the cultural Third, but the Home Service and sometimes the Light Programme when the musical content was suitable.

When Malcolm Sargent took over the conductorship in 1950, the Proms found a showman to match this moment of post-war confidence. The big innovation

of the 1950s was television, and that played perfectly to Sargent's skills. For Henry Wood the Last Night of the Proms had been a traditional occasion, but the fun was restricted to Wood's donning more and more of his going-home clothes – coat, hat and umbrella – as the applause resounded. Sargent and the BBC saw the potential of the visual medium, and there was a radical change from the sober Albert Hall photographed at the end of the 1947 season under Adrian Boult *(see left)*, to an ever more vivid display of flags and nationalist enthusiasm. Sargent arranged a new version of Arne's 'Rule, Britannia!' for soloist and orchestra (Wood's original 1905 *Fantasia on British Sea-Songs* had included only an orchestral version), for which a generation of leading British singers has created more and more lively costumes.

66 Through being relayed to a wider public, the Proms season took its place alongside sporting, royal and ceremonial occasions as one of the landmarks of British national life. 99

Television became an ever more essential part of disseminating the Proms as new free-to-air digital channels were originated (remember BBC Knowledge, the forerunner of BBC Four?), and so too did the internet. The global reach of the Proms expanded in a way that Henry Wood could only have dreamt of,

Intergalactic reach: a Dalek storms the first Doctor Who Prom in 2008, conducted by Murray Gold (composer of music for the series from 2005 to 2017): the event featured the screening of a new mini-episode featuring the 10th Doctor, David Tennant, who also appeared live onstage

and the educative intent of the original partnership between the BBC and the Proms was demonstrated by background talks and events, educational projects, and much later specially created events for younger audiences based on BBC brands such as *Blue Peter* and *Doctor Who*. Daleks in the Albert Hall shocked some, but they offered a way into the concerts for a new generation who had not been brought up on classical music. Participation became ever more vital an element; greater diversity and non-Western music became a regularly established feature of the season.

A decisive move forwards in the partnership between technology and broadcasting came with the innovation of BBC Proms in the Park in 1996, using the development of big screens to relay the climax of the Last Night's concert

first into Hyde Park, and then in the following years to centres around the UK, with musical inserts from the nations, so that the occasion was turned into a genuinely national celebration. Now the growing popularity of BBC iPlayer and BBC Sounds has enabled audiences to access the Proms whenever and wherever they want. Who knows what innovations future seasons may bring?

There is one very simple symbol of how the partnership of the Henry Wood Promenade Concerts and the British Broadcasting Corporation has come together, and that is their name in recent decades. The 'BBC Proms' brings together this artistically adventurous concert season with the sustaining power of broadcasting. As a result, the Proms has had powerful and far-reaching effects on the development of music in this country, supporting composers and performers, providing opportunities for new and established talent, and welcoming artists from around the world. It is the security of funding provided by the BBC through the licence fee, the commitment to the highest standards of rehearsal and performance and the continuing investment that involves, that has ensured the distinctive mixture of quality and popularity that marks out the Proms as something uniquely valuable in our flourishing musical life. ●

Nicholas Kenyon was Director of the BBC Proms (1996 to 2007) and Managing Director of London's Barbican Centre (2007–21). He is now Opera Critic of the *Telegraph* and a Visiting Scholar of the Faculty of Music, Cambridge University. He was the consultant editor of *The Proms: A New History* (Thames and Hudson, 2007).

Mozart
at Close Quarters

As Leif Ove Andsnes and the Mahler Chamber
Orchestra bring their Mozart Momentum series to the
Proms, exploring key works written in the years 1785
and 1786, NICHOLAS BARAGWANATH talks to the pianist
about this especially fruitful period in Mozart's output

n 2015 Norwegian star pianist Leif Ove Andsnes and the Mahler Chamber Orchestra concluded their four-year Beethoven Journey, exploring all five of Beethoven's piano concertos on an international tour, including at the Proms. Their latest multi-year project, again with Andsnes featuring as both soloist and director, centres on Mozart and the years 1785–6, in which, at the height of his powers, he pushed the boundaries of both dramatic and intimate expression.

Aptly enough, the first concerto to be heard in this summer's three Mozart Momentum Proms (two orchestral, one chamber) is the D minor Concerto (No. 20). This was the work with which Andsnes made his public concerto debut, at the age of 14. He remembers the sound of the orchestra swirling around him 'like a roaring animal' and, he says, 'I've been hooked ever since!' But this concerto is special for another reason. For Andsnes, it marks the beginning of a new creative phase for Mozart. 'It introduces a previously unheard level of musical storytelling.' In these concerts, his aim is to bring these stories to life.

Mozart wrote the D minor Concerto in 1785 for that year's Lenten concert season in Vienna. From the start, the audience must have realised they were

◀ Multitasking in Mozart: pianist and director Leif Ove Andsnes in a Mozart Momentum performance with the Mahler Chamber Orchestra at Hamburg's Elbphilharmonie last year

being treated to something special. The orchestra begins with a dark, stormy theme, full of sobbing syncopation and chromatic pathos. It builds up to a forceful outburst of dotted martial rhythms, ready for the hero – the soloist – to make an entrance with an impressive flourish or an embellished retelling of the story. But, in an extraordinary gesture, Mozart began the solo arrival with completely new material. 'That's totally radical,' says Andsnes. By convention, the soloist would begin by elaborating on the music the orchestra had played in the introduction.' This opening piano melody aches with quiet despair. It comes across as an individual's reflection on what has gone before. It's a 'lonely subject', Andsnes says, standing apart from nature and society, of a type that was to become a standard trope in later, Romantic works. It perhaps helps to explain why this was one of Beethoven's favourite concertos.

In the first of his three Proms with the MCO, Andsnes pairs this brooding D minor Concerto with a brighter work, the Piano Concerto No. 22 in E flat major, with which Mozart opened the following Lenten season in 1786. 'Like many of Mozart's works from that year,' Andsnes comments, 'there's so much theatre, so much opera. You can feel the different characters from the beginning.' In fact, there are so many contrasting voices that at times it is difficult to identify one as more prominent than the others: 'The web of themes is so complex that it leads one to ask: Is this the melody, or is that?'

Andsnes praises not only the cleverness of this music, but also its warmth, charm and generosity. Speaking of the concerto's beautiful slow movement, he describes how it seems 'so full of soul, in a way that only Mozart can create; it plays with light and darkness and at the same time seems to caress you'. The ebullient final movement, by contrast, invites us to revel in the interplay of hunting horns, country jigs and echoing bird calls.

Although Mozart did not invent the piano concerto, he made it his own. He used it as a vehicle both for his dramatic talent and his virtuosity – in the original sense of possessing the 'virtues' of knowledge and inventive skill, as opposed to just technical facility. Andsnes emphasises that each concerto should be heard as a kind of mini opera, with the pianist as the main character in dialogue with a host of orchestral voices. In Mozart's hands, the concerto had by now become a profound social drama, in which the soloist and orchestra enacted a metaphorical play on the individual's relationship to society. This was boosted by the concerto's ambiguous position, falling between public and private spheres and possessing attributes both of the large-scale concert and of the more intimate salon, albeit for paying subscribers. True to the ideals of the Enlightenment, the archetypal trajectory of the individual movements runs from competition and disagreement through dramatic dialogue to eventual cooperation and reconciliation.

This strategy can be heard in the work that Andsnes has chosen to end his

The Burgtheater in Vienna's St Michaelsplatz, where Mozart's Piano Concerto No. 24 was thought until recently to have been premiered, and which saw the first performances of three of Mozart's operas, including *The Marriage of Figaro*

second Mozart Momentum concert, the Piano Concerto No. 24 in C minor. It opens with a forceful orchestral statement, at once proud and portentous, that draws its strength from hints of ancient fugue and French overture. When the soloist enters with a completely new theme – 'so simple, genuine and heartfelt,' Andsnes says – it dissipates the might of the social (orchestral) order and replaces its bombast with the voice of the individual (soloist).

The C minor Concerto, now thought to have been performed at the academy held at Vienna's Kärntnertor Theatre in April 1786, marked the end of Mozart's run as a performer-impresario. His thoughts had already begun to turn to opera and, in particular, to *The Marriage of Figaro*. Some speculate that he may have wanted to move away from his public image as a virtuoso performer and to be regarded more as a Kapellmeister (court composer), on an equal footing with the Italian maestros such as Salieri and Paisiello, whose works dominated Vienna's opera theatres. Others suggest that he may have been forced to limit his performing career after suffering injury to his hands from overuse. Whatever the reason, in *Figaro* he achieved the goal he had set himself in the piano concertos: to create music of supreme quality that was at the same time genuinely popular.

The overture to *The Marriage of Figaro* testifies to his success. It encapsulates the entire drama. From the opening flurry of notes, it depicts the bawdy, boisterous action that will entangle servants and masters, plotters and accomplices in a

series of intrigues that eventually result in reconciliation and shared humanity. The music portrays the many characters of the drama, from the rustic dances and chromatic innuendos of lowly peasants to the formal minuets of the aristocracy, and undergoes as many twists and turns as the plot. It bears witness to Andsnes's claim that Mozart's music of these years creates a new kind of storytelling.

As well as being warmly received in Vienna, *The Marriage of Figaro* was a huge hit in Prague. Alert as ever for opportunities to make a profit, Mozart decided to capitalise on the interest by embarking on a tour to the Czech capital. He wrote his celebrated 'Prague' Symphony (No. 38) in late 1786, specially for an academy to be held at the National Theatre, at which he would also play three piano improvisations. The symphony is one of Mozart's grandest creations, a hymn of thanks to the Czech people for their support and understanding. Its slow introduction frames the heroic action of the first movement, while the slow movement offers nostalgic reminiscences of a lost idyll, intensified with expressions of painful memories in minor-key outbursts. The finale dispels the tension with bustling activity.

In Vienna, Mozart was in high demand among the wealthy, leisured classes as performer, composer and teacher. His work rate was incredible. Yet he found time to join the Freemasons, quickly rising to the highest rank of Master Mason. He was an active and enthusiastic participant and composed much music for the order. The *Masonic Funeral Music* was composed in late 1785 for memorial services at the 'Crowned Hope' Lodge for two brothers, Duke Georg von Mecklenburg and Count Franz Esterházy. Mozart received a eulogy at this same Lodge on his passing. The funeral music suggests a wealth of number symbolism and hidden meaning, as embodied in the mysterious four pairs of opening chords, which establish a suitably solemn mood.

As he approached his 30th birthday in 1786, Mozart was at the peak of his fame and creative powers. His decision to quit a secure but servile position in Salzburg for a freelance career in Vienna had been proved right. After several anxious years winning over aristocratic patrons and gaining favour with the Viennese court, he could finally start to relax and to indulge his creativity to the full. This new sense of confidence can be heard in the works composed in 1785 and 1786, which rank among his greatest achievements. ●

Nicholas Baragwanath is a pianist and academic who studied piano at the Royal Academy of Music and Royal Northern College of Music. He is a professor at Nottingham University, with research interests spanning the Renaissance to the present day. He appears regularly on BBC Radio 3, Radio 4 and the World Service.

The Marriage of Figaro – overture; Piano Concertos Nos. 20 and 22
PROM 28 • 7 AUGUST, 3.00pm

Symphony No. 38, 'Prague'; songs; Concert aria 'Ch'io mi scordi di te?'; Masonic Funeral Music; Piano Concerto No. 24
PROM 29 • 7 AUGUST, 7.30pm

Piano Trio in B flat major; Piano Quartet in E flat major
PROMS AT BATTERSEA • 8 AUGUST, 1.00pm

Mozart from the Inside

Matthew Truscott, concertmaster of the Mahler Chamber Orchestra, offers a player's view of getting to grips with Mozart and working with Leif Ove Andsnes

Our Beethoven Journey collaboration with Leif Ove Andsnes culminated at the Proms in 2015 and it redefined how we felt about ourselves as an orchestra. This was the first project of its kind for the Mahler Chamber Orchestra, the idea being to develop an artistic relationship over a number of years and to focus on particular repertoire. The fruits of this project have been rich and lasting: not only the inspiration for a new artistic structure for the orchestra but also our deep and precious relationship with Leif Ove.

The planning for Mozart Momentum started almost as soon as the Beethoven Journey had ended. Leif Ove's concept of focusing on 1785–6 as a particularly prolific period in Mozart's life was irresistible for what it offered in terms of exploring the increasingly radical piano music of this period and also the wider context of Mozart's orchestral writing.

Living with this music for the past couple of years has allowed the time to reflect not only on its startling brilliance but also its consistent invention and variety. In every moment Mozart seems to create and recreate with total command, manipulating his material and his elusively wonderful orchestral textures in ways that can suddenly undo you with their power, their delicacy or their emotional resonance. The overture to *The Marriage of Figaro* and the *Masonic Funeral Music* couldn't be any more different, for instance, but they both refer in a heartfelt and direct way to the human condition.

There's a special individual responsibility in Classical-period repertoire to play with clarity and to listen hard. This is something the orchestra prides itself on, and has been over the years the platform for our most exhilarating moments together. It is particularly satisfying as an orchestral musician that these practical requirements are also the means by which this music is rendered at its most crystalline and luminous.

Leif Ove makes the ideal partner in this endeavour, producing playing and inspiration that is at all times not only clear and striking, but which has humility and generosity at its core. He encourages and celebrates the easy exchange among all the musicians on stage, among whom, miraculously, he considers himself an equal partner.

The project has coincided with the Covid pandemic in a way that has stymied some of our aspirations but at the same time increased the potency of what we have managed to achieve. Often over the past couple of years there have been moments where it has felt like an extraordinary, wide-eyed privilege to be in a room with these dear colleagues and this repertoire. Better still are the occasions when the presence of an audience completes the wonderful communion that is live music-making.

Sounds *Electric*

Over a century after its invention, the theremin makes its first concerto appearance at the Proms – along with a handful of other instruments that have evaded the solo limelight. The swooping, other-worldly sounds of this pioneering electrical instrument have captured the imaginations of composers and audiences alike, says Radio 3's ELIZABETH ALKER

To see the theremin played is as eerie and wonderful an experience as it is to hear the sound the instrument makes. Its unearthly whine and vibrato wail are as mysterious as the sight of a thereminist conjuring these spectral noises out of thin air. You'd be forgiven for thinking that wizardry was involved – and for a long time people believed exactly that. In popular culture the theremin is the sound of phantom or extraterrestrial activity, as we hear in the scores of 1950s sci-fi movies such as *The Day the Earth Stood Still*. Its disembodied howl has also signified psychological torment and existential crisis, as heard in Miklós Rózsa's music for Billy Wilder's *The Lost Weekend* and Hitchcock's *Spellbound*, both released in 1945.

The story of the theremin is just as extraordinary as the instrument sounds and looks. It started life 102 years ago in St Petersburg, where the 23-year-old scientist Lev Sergeyevich Termen (later to be known as Léon Theremin) had been recruited by Lenin's newly formed Bolshevik government. Theremin's educational background was unusual. He held a degree in both cello performance and physics, but it was his scientific knowledge and thirst for invention that Soviet officials believed would be of most value to the regime. He was employed in the newly established Physico-Technical

◀ The original air instrument, played by Lithuanian-born violinist and thereminist Clara Rockmore (1911–98) in New York, 1936

Institute, a centre for covert strategies, and it was here, as head of the 'high-frequency oscillations' laboratory, that his career in espionage began. Theremin went on to create sophisticated listening devices, such as an antenna to be hidden in the US ambassador's Moscow office and the famous Buran eavesdropping system, which used an infrared beam to detect patterns of conversation through glass.

> 66 In popular culture the theremin is the sound of phantom or extraterrestrial activity, as we hear in the scores of 1950s sci-fi movies such as *The Day the Earth Stood Still*. 99

It was in the early days of his tenure at the Institute that Theremin began building a device intended to measure the density of gas. As an experiment, he added an audion oscillator – a gadget that generates sound. This made a whistling noise that would alter according to the density of the gases measured by the meter on the device. He soon realised that, when he put his hand near the device, it interfered with the meter reading and altered the tone produced by the audion oscillator. Albert Glinsky, author of *Theremin: Ether Music and Espionage*, refers to this phenomenon as 'capacitance'. The dormant cellist inside Theremin was awoken and, since he was able to control the pitch of the oscillator with his hands, he immediately

saw its musical potential. The minds of his fellow employees boggled as they watched him strum thin air, pulling notes out of nothingness and making electricity sing with his bare hands.

The new instrument was named an 'ethertone', and in October 1920, after some modification, it was ready for its first public demonstration. Students at the Institute gathered for a rendition of 'The Swan' from Saint-Saëns's *The Carnival of the Animals*, extracts from Minkus's ballet *Fiammetta* and Massenet's *Élégie*. Word of the ethertone quickly spread and, before long, a clapped-out old Austin was sent from the Kremlin to take Theremin for an audience with Lenin. It seems that even the architect of one of the bloodiest acts of regicide in history could be rendered affable by this new musical magic trick. Theremin described Lenin as 'a very nice and pleasant person' who enjoyed his ethertone performance of a Scriabin *Étude* so much that he wanted a go on the device himself. Theremin took the Russian leader's hands and together they played Glinka's *The Lark*. So impressed was Lenin that a free rail pass was issued for Theremin, and the new superstar inventor was sent around the country on an agitprop tour, tasked with showing off this latest Soviet achievement and persuading the masses of the advantages that electricity and modernity could bring.

In 1927 Theremin made his way to New York City. Here he patented his device and, two years later, the American electronics company RCA offered him $100,000 to manufacture it themselves.

They naively believed it was something that everybody could learn to play. In reality, there were so many external factors affecting its sound – the temperature of the thereminist's hands, the room's humidity and the proximity of other performers or the audience – that mastering the instrument proved extremely difficult.

Theremin's subsequent time in America saw him rub shoulders with Albert Einstein and marry the African American prima ballerina Lavinia Williams. As the Second World War approached, however, his background in Russian espionage and mounting debts caught up with him and he was forced to make a sudden escape. Returning to an even more hostile Stalinist Russia, though, he soon found himself a political prisoner in one of the most brutal and remotely situated Gulags in Siberia. He didn't visit the USA again until 1991, but during his absence his instrument took on a life of its own, becoming a mainstay of Hollywood sci-fi thrillers and a popular lounge jazz instrument. It was also the first and last love of synth inventor and electronic music pioneer Robert Moog. As a young man in the mid-1950s Moog developed home theremin kits and sold them via mail order out of his childhood home in Queens.

Over a century after its invention, leading thereminist Carolina Eyck believes there is renewed interest in the instrument, led by a hipster fondness for retro technology. She also believes contemporary composition for the theremin has moved

it away from its sci-fi association. New writing for the instrument requires, in her words, 'a cleaner, higher sound and virtuosic skill'. She names works by German composer Christopher Tarnow and French composer Régis Campo as fine examples of new pieces for the instrument. These, alongside Finnish composer Kalevi Aho's Theremin Concerto *Eight Seasons*, which Eyck (its dedicatee) will perform at this year's Proms. Eyck also writes her own music – a blissful combination of the rich and earthy sound of her voice and the soaring, mystical sonorities of the theremin.

The way the theremin is written into music and popular culture might have changed, but Eyck believes audiences have never lost their sense of awe and wonder at the sight of one being played. 'This instrument is over 100 years old,' she says, 'but people still think it's magical. My father put me on the stage when I was very little, and to play this instrument made me feel so free, physically and mentally. People would ask if I was a magician and that is when I knew the theremin was my thing.' ●

Elizabeth Alker is a broadcaster and writer who has presented for BBC Radio 6 Music and currently presents *Saturday Breakfast* and *Unclassified* for BBC Radio 3.

Kalevi Aho Eight Seasons (Concerto for Theremin and Chamber Orchestra)
PROM 25 • 4 AUGUST

See also concertos for flute (Prom 2), viola (Proms 5 & 65), harp (Prom 9), percussion (Prom 18), tuba (Prom 39) and trombone (Prom 40)

From Another World

Composer Danny Elfman (whose new piece is heard in Prom 27) recalls the first time he heard the theremin

I first heard the theremin while watching a mid-1960s re-release of *The Day the Earth Stood Still*, which has music by Bernard Herrmann. I must have been about 11 or 12 years old and, for the first time, I became aware that the music I was hearing did not simply *exist*, but also had the power to engage my imagination and enhance my appreciation of the movie I was watching. That movie – and that score – is responsible for my lifelong infatuation with film music.

Of course, the theremin became a big part of the 'sci-fi sound' in that era, but I later learnt that Miklós Rózsa had been experimenting with the instrument as early as 1945 in his score to *The Lost Weekend*. I think my favourite use of the theremin is in Dimitri Tiomkin's music for Howard Hawks's 1951 horror classic *The Thing from Another World*. Wow! That nasty growl he managed to get out of the instrument was absolutely perfect!

In 1996 I finally got to let loose with the theremin in my score for Tim Burton's *Mars Attacks!*. It felt as though I was doing my part to keep the great theremin tradition alive!

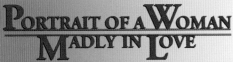

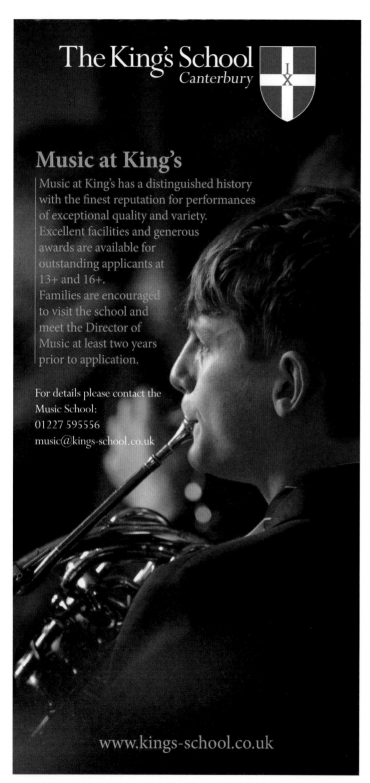

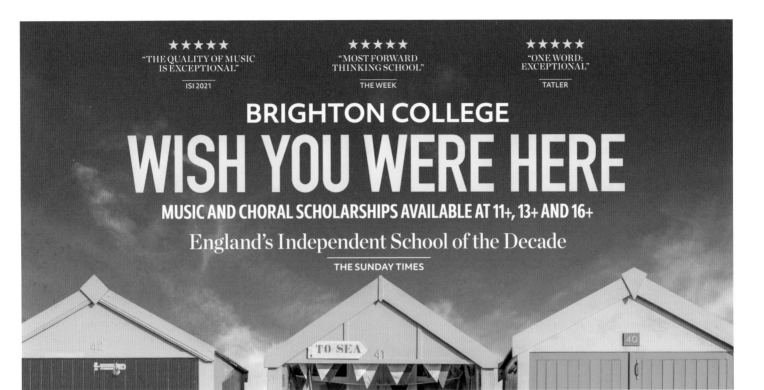

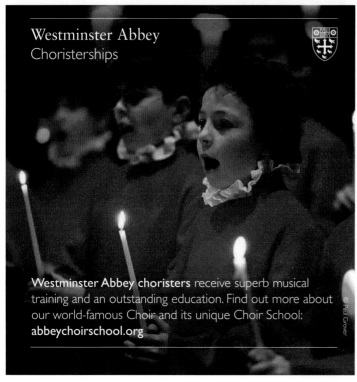

Full Steam Ahead

After the disruption of the Covid-19 pandemic, and in the light of environmental concerns, many orchestras are reassessing their approach to touring. JESSICA DUCHEN takes stock of the various challenges they now face, and asks what we stand to lose if those international connections are broken

◀ All abroad: train travel is becoming an increasingly important mode of transport for orchestras and soloists on tour

I f you thought that the UK music scene had experienced a 'perfect storm' these past few years, you wouldn't be wrong. It is hard to imagine a time quite so challenging on so many fronts. The fact that the Proms is happening at all is testimony to the creativity, ingenuity and sheer dogged determination of everyone involved – especially so when it comes to orchestras on tour.

The global music industry is predicated on ease of international travel and the presentation of live events for large audiences, perhaps the areas hardest hit by the simultaneous challenges of the Covid-19 pandemic, climate change and new regulations following Brexit. Environmental responsibility is now a key investment principle in certain arts funding programmes, adding extra pressure. It is almost impossible to disentangle one set of challenges from another and finding a silver lining is not easy. Mark Pemberton, Director of the Association of British Orchestras, has been a key figure in keeping UK orchestral life on the rails. 'We've been in perpetual crisis mode,' he says. 'Right now, it's all about survival.' Touring is both part of the problem and part of the solution.

Undoubtedly there are benefits in orchestral touring: not least, orchestras are a British export success. 'Our government is keen on "soft power" and British orchestras fly the flag abroad. They go out and export their excellence,' says Pemberton. 'Promoters overseas will pay for that, so they bring money back into the UK. We also love to welcome orchestras from abroad here. It's all part of showcasing the best of classical music, which is also why the Proms exists.' The BBC Symphony Orchestra's Tours Manager, Kathryn Aldersea, agrees. 'We are very much ambassadors for the BBC – it is a global organisation with an international presence, and we go abroad to perform for that worldwide audience directly.'

But there are also upsides to cutting down on touring. Each day away adds significantly to the cost, so most groups have little alternative to same-day travel and concert, with red-eye flights and little time to rest or eat. Is it really worth the stress, never mind the carbon footprint? 'Maybe one should question the wisdom of flying orchestras of 100 people and crew between continents to effectively play the same works,' says Pemberton. Yet when, for instance, the BBC SO plays British music abroad, while the Philadelphia Orchestra, visiting the Proms, performs Florence Price and Valerie Coleman with the soprano Angel Blue, the advantages become clearer, enriching the audience experience and displaying part of a national culture.

During the pandemic, though, short-notice cancellations have been legion. Covid regulations have varied between countries, often changing rapidly, disrupting tours that were planned months or longer in advance. Managers face dilemmas when, for instance, a couple of dates on a week-long tour vanish due to sudden shifts in local restrictions. Earlier this season, whole trips occasionally bit the dust when a couple of players tested positive for Covid; and, if the players are salaried, or freelance but cancelled at short notice, they would usually still be paid, the orchestra bearing the cost. Sometimes players have caught Covid on tour and have had to self-isolate in a hotel room for two weeks – a situation with a raft of other implications.

> " Realistically, we might have to be a bit more local, but let's not lose the prize of the international connections. We're an international art form: we still want to tour, but to do so responsibly. "

Dame Sarah Connolly, one of the UK's most sought-after mezzo-sopranos, says that the risks can be overwhelming. 'Supposing I accept an opera in Spain,' she says, 'and then I test positive on the day of my first performance? I then have to isolate for two weeks. If the run is only for two weeks, I lose my whole fee, because they have to pay a replacement, and there's no insurance. The fear of losing earnings is enormous.'

Hovering over these conundrums is the spectre of environmental responsibility, now mandatory for funding investment. 'Nobody wants a situation where we're not allowing orchestras to go on tour,'

> **" The pandemic has given us an opportunity to rethink the way we are planning and working. In the last decade a lot of the most successful work that we've done is when we've had time to build relationships, to engage with the artists and audiences, and we haven't just been obsessed with catching the next plane. With longer residencies, you stay in one place for a significant amount of time. Artistically it's better and environmentally it's better.**

Kathryn McDowell, Managing Director of the London Symphony Orchestra, speaking of the benefits of extending orchestral touring periods on Radio 3's *Music Matters* last November

Pemberton says. 'Realistically, we might have to be a bit more local, but let's not lose the prize of the international connections. We're an international art form: we still want to tour abroad, but to do so responsibly.'

Some orchestras have committed to travelling by train whenever possible – as the Orchestra of the Age of Enlightenment did for its tour to Poland and Hungary last year – and increased rail links to places such as Amsterdam and northern Germany are proving valuable. In the season ahead, the OAE is hatching an ambitious plan to travel by train as far as China, playing in as many places as possible en route. 'Many journeys are completely feasible by train,' says its Chief Executive, Crispin Woodhead. 'Although it takes longer, it is better for everybody, including the players' health.'

Nevertheless, joined-up thinking in the travel industry would help, Aldersea says: 'Currently you can book flights 11 months in advance. With trains, it is only three months. That really does complicate things.' Taking an orchestra between London and the Mediterranean coast costs about the same by train as by air. 'But a full day of travel instead of half a day increases the per diem payments.' A few busy soloists are considering taking on less work, or opting for railway travel. Others inevitably prioritise their own survival. As Connolly points out, many young singers in the early stages of their careers rely on overseas opportunities to help pay the bills at home.

Might some tours be replaced by digital streaming? 'Developments in digital that could have taken 10 years have happened in one year, because they had to,' says Pemberton. The BBC SO found that contributing filmed material for festivals they could not visit physically helped to maintain presence; at the Kissinger Sommer festival in Germany, the orchestra even expanded its ongoing education work. 'We perhaps had a wider reach than if we'd done the project in "real life",' Aldersea notes. However, having decided to stream this material for free, the BBC SO received no financial benefit. 'Digital does not replace the income generated by live events,' says Pemberton, 'so it will always be an add-on.' As for audiences, Aldersea acknowledges, 'Nothing can replace the live experience of music.'

Brexit is another consideration. Being a 'third country' means more red tape for British artists touring to Europe. 'We are navigating 27 different visa and work permit regimes and across the board there's additional customs paperwork and increased costs,' says Pemberton. The road haulage issue – 'cabotage' – is one such example. A UK HGV can only make a limited number of stops in the EU: 'So a UK orchestra can't use its own truck in multi-date tours.'

Old patterns of touring are unlikely to return and creative solutions are badly needed; and, while there is no shortage of ideas, implementation is the big challenge. Building for the future, Connolly wants to encourage more young people who are passionate about music to go into arts management and find those solutions: 'There are some excellent university courses,' she says.

Despite the complications around touring, Pemberton maintains optimism. 'British orchestras have always been enterprising and found a way,' he says. 'We remain popular abroad and, equally, our great festivals, like the Proms, will still be as welcoming to foreign orchestras as they have always been. Then we will remain an art form whereby we learn from each other and exchange the best.' ●

Jessica Duchen's music journalism has appeared in *BBC Music Magazine*, *The Independent* and *The Sunday Times*. She is the author of seven novels, two plays, biographies of Korngold and Fauré and the libretto for Roxanna Panufnik's opera *Silver Birch*.

Stateside Story

Matías Tarnopolsky, President and CEO of the Philadelphia Orchestra and Kimmel Center, asks what it means for a US orchestra to tour in 2022

International touring has been part of the Philadelphia Orchestra's DNA since 1918, when it first crossed the border into Canada. The idea of an orchestra as a cultural ambassador is incredibly powerful, and the Philadelphia Orchestra has been a leader in this regard: it was the first US orchestra to travel to China, in 1973, six years before there were diplomatic relations between the two countries. The human connections made on that trip are now in their third and fourth generations. It's the most extraordinary thing to meet people, as I have done, who say: 'My parents went to that concert. I was 6 years old and had to stay at home. It was the only subject of conversation around our dinner table growing up, so for me to see the orchestra with my own children is very special.' These stories are repeated to us by audiences around the world.

So, when we look at the issue through a contemporary lens, we have to ask ourselves: 'What does it mean to tour in 2022?' The importance of cultural exchange, of connecting with audiences around the world, remains undiminished. In fact, it's probably more important now than ever before. Music can give voice to thoughts and ideas that words alone cannot. Amid the nationwide reckoning over long-present issues of systemic racism, inequality and injustice, we felt it was our duty to respond in the only way we know how: through music. Hence why you see composers such as Valerie Coleman, Florence Price, Jessie Montgomery and countless others featured prominently in our programmes. That's just one example of the numerous ways in which the orchestra has been using its voice as a public advocate for justice. Our entire season has been informed and transformed by the impact of the pandemic, the social justice movement in America and the drive toward creative equity and inclusion in the world of orchestral music – and you will see that reflected in our tour repertoire as well.

At the same time, we need to take very seriously our responsibility as a public cultural institution to preserve our fragile environment. To that end, during the pandemic we adjusted our touring model to include multi-concert residencies, meaning less travel between stops; we reduced the size of the touring party and built brand-new, environmentally efficient wardrobe trunks for the orchestra; we also travel by train or bus whenever possible. Environmentalism is central to the conversation in ways that it wasn't a decade ago. It's long overdue. But we must also remember that music, too, can be a force for change. There's nothing quite like that moment of connection and contemplation, when you're standing in the Arena at the Proms, in front of one of the truly great world orchestras, like I did as a teenager. It opens doors into new ways of thinking. And I hope one of those doors is: 'What can I do to make the world a better place?'

Behold *... The Sea!*

Whether inspired by its dazzling reflections, restless energy or unfathomable depths, composers – as well as painters and poets – have been enthralled by the sea for centuries. RICHARD HAMBLYN steers a course through its symbolism and allure

On a summer afternoon in 1789 a bare-legged George III stepped nervously into the sea at Weymouth to the strains of the National Anthem performed by a small chamber orchestra huddled in a nearby 'bathing machine'. The modern seaside holiday had arrived. Considering the degree to which British culture has been shaped by the sea throughout its history, it's surprising that it took so long, but then the sea has been a place of work far longer than a site of leisure, an unforgiving taskscape marked by its own musical legacies of shanties and shipwreck ballads. By the time Claude Debussy rented a room at the Grand Hotel, Eastbourne, in the summer of 1905, however, the southern English coastline had been comprehensively tamed. 'The sea unfurls itself with an utterly British correctness … what a place for working in!' he wrote, going on to complain that there were 'too many draughts and too much music, both of which I try to avoid'.

Debussy had come to Eastbourne from Paris partly to escape the scandal of his impending divorce, and partly to devote himself to the three 'symphonic sketches' that would become one of his best-known works: *La mer*. Proximity to the sea seemed to sharpen his focus for,

during the earlier stages of composition, Debussy had resisted visiting the coast, preferring to draw on half-remembered seaside visions from childhood trips to Brittany. 'The sea fascinates me to the point of paralysing my creative faculties,' he said, claiming that he had never been able to write a note in the presence of the sea itself. But it was in Eastbourne that he eventually settled on the final arrangement of *La mer*, naming its three movements 'De l'aube à midi sur la mer' (From Dawn to Midday on the Sea), 'Jeux de vagues' (Play of the Waves) and 'Dialogue du vent et de la mer' (Dialogue of the Wind and the Sea). The programme notes for the premiere, given later that year in Paris, likened *La mer* to a painting, observing that the orchestral effects of the piece were achieved through 'a palette of sounds and brushstrokes designed to convey in gradations of rare and brilliant colours the play of light and shade and the chiaroscuro of the ever-changing seascape'.

The comparison between music and painting was apposite, the heyday of early 20th-century sea music having arisen partly in response to the universal popularity of the painted (and photographed) seascape. In a chapter entitled 'The Truth of Water' in his influential study *Modern Painters* (1843), the art critic John Ruskin had argued that the sea poses a particular challenge to artistic representation, its restless turbulence being too often conveyed as mere formless disorder. 'The sea *must* be legitimately drawn,' he chided; 'it

cannot be given as utterly disorganised and confused', and he urged artists of all kinds to pay close attention to what he called the sea's essential 'fury and formalism'. His advice may have been aimed primarily at visual artists, but it is in that very combination of 'fury' and 'formalism' that composers possess the advantage of representing, however obliquely, the sea's perpetual transformations of mood and movement.

> 66 Fom the British perspective, the sea, once the great conduit of Empire, was turning into a defensive moat, alive with fantasies of siege and invasion, whether by foreign powers or, more recently, by boatloads of desperate migrants. 99

Many of the concert repertoire's best-loved sea-pieces appeared over the course of a single musically intense decade, encompassing, alongside *La mer* itself (1903–5), Elgar's *Sea Pictures* (1899), Ethel Smyth's *The Wreckers* (1902–4), Delius's *Sea Drift* (1903–4), Stanford's *Songs of the Sea* (1904), Vaughan Williams's *A Sea Symphony* (1903–9) and Frank Bridge's *The Sea* (1910–11), the last written in an Eastbourne hotel in avowed emulation of Debussy. Bridge's nautical tone-poem would be the first piece of modern music encountered by a 10-year-old Benjamin Britten, whose later

◀ Wreckers off the coast of Northumberland, as imagined by J. M. W. Turner in 1833–4; Ethel Smyth's opera *The Wreckers* takes place 'on the wildest part of the Cornish coast'

'Sea Interludes' from *Peter Grimes* (1945) owed much to his teacher's example.

But there was a dark side to that maritime decade, for the years leading up to the First World War had seen the European powers begin to build up their fleets, while Britain's once-feted naval supremacy – 'Britannia, rule the waves!' (as first sung in Arne's masque *Alfred* of 1740) – continued its post-Napoleonic decline, leading to widespread fears of invasion. Those fears were memorably articulated in Erskine Childers's bestselling novel *The Riddle of the Sands* (1903), while Stanford's patriotic *Songs of the Fleet* (1910) expressed them in musical form.

From the British perspective, the surrounding sea, once the great conduit of Empire, was turning into a defensive moat, alive with atavistic fantasies of siege and invasion, whether by foreign powers or, more recently, by boatloads of desperate migrants. For the Swiss-born Carl Jung, who accompanied Sigmund Freud on his first Atlantic crossing in the summer of 1909, the sea supplied a ready symbol of the deep unconscious, a source of fearful fascination as well as an elemental threshold that can never be lightly crossed. 'The sea is like music,' Jung declared in his journal; 'it has all the dreams of the soul within itself and sounds them over.' Like the seven voyages

of Sinbad, as narrated in the *One Thousand and One Nights*, every journey over the sea is a journey into the unknown.

For Sinbad, who survives multiple shipwrecks, storms and kidnappings, the sea was the site of violent transformation, as can be heard in the dramatic finale of Rimsky-Korsakov's *Scheherazade* (1888), in which Sinbad's ship is driven onto the waiting rocks by furious storm-waves. The composer drew from personal experience as much as from folklore, his self-described poetic love of the sea having prompted him to join the Imperial Russian Navy at the age of 12. For years he combined his love of music with his life at sea, composing whenever off-watch, sourcing manuscript paper during spells of shore leave, even installing an upright piano in his cramped midshipman's cabin. Though Rimsky-Korsakov had retired from the navy by the time he came to write *Scheherazade,* salt water runs through all four movements, the orchestral crashing of the waves alternating with delicate passages for solo instruments, the orchestration growing fuller and richer each time the 'waves' reappear, swelling like the sea itself as it rushes towards the land.

Of course, there is more to sea-themed music than onomatopoeia. Ethel Smyth's *The Wreckers* had its origin in stories of 'false lights' wrecking along the Cornish coast, the three-act opera telling a murderous tale of plunder and heroism, while Vaughan Williams's *A Sea Symphony* was rooted more in folk song and Walt Whitman's *Leaves of Grass*

(from which the choral texts were drawn) than in any programmatic attempt to render the sounds of the sea. But later composers, such as Grace Williams, who had been one of Vaughan Williams's pupils at the Royal College of Music, discovered a renewed enthusiasm for the sonically descriptive seascape. Her *Sea Sketches* (1944), a suite of five movements for string orchestra, explored her near-somatic relationship with the sea – 'What I really want, and have always wanted, is to live near the sea: if only I could have a month at sea I'd be a new woman,' she wrote – and much of her music, notably the five *Sea Sketches*, sought to channel the sounds and rhythms of the sea in its various moods, from the forceful rolling of the tide in 'Breakers', to the mournful reverberation of a foghorn in 'Channel Sirens', sounded, via the cellos' bass notes, through the spectral sea mists evoked on the violas' upper strings.

What these sketches convey so clearly is the sea's inexhaustible energy. When an incoming wave breaks on the shore, it appears as though the water has come to the end of a long journey, when in fact the water itself has hardly moved. Wind-driven sea waves transmit kinetic energy, not water, and the turbulence in the swash zone is the result of that energy encountering an obstruction – usually the shelving sea floor – against which it noisily dissipates; though, in the case of Doreen Carwithen's *Bishop Rock* overture (1952), that obstacle is the Bishop Rock lighthouse, the westernmost point of England, on the edge of the Scilly Isles,

some 30 miles off Land's End. The piece begins with the swirling, dashing sound of powerful waves hitting the lighthouse, horns and trombones blaring, before the sea slowly calms to a steady, reflective quiescence.

As do all the dazzling sea pieces that feature in this year's Proms season, *Bishop Rock* pays haunting testament to a deep-seated creative and emotional response to what Debussy called 'this great blue sphinx': the unfathomable sea, at once timeless and nostalgic, where all that is familiar ends and the vast unknown begins. ●

Richard Hamblyn is an environmental writer and historian whose most recent book is *The Sea: Nature and Culture* (2021). Other titles include *Clouds: Nature and Culture* (2017), *The Invention of Clouds* (2002, which won the 2002 *Los Angeles Times* Book Prize) and *Terra: Tales of the Earth* (2009). He is a Senior Lecturer in the Department of English at Birkbeck, University of London.

Rimsky-Korsakov Scheherezade
PROM 9 • 21 JULY

CBeebies Prom: A Journey into the Ocean
PROMS 11 & 12 • 23 JULY

Smyth The Wreckers
PROM 13 • 24 JULY

Carwithen Bishop Rock
Grace Williams Sea Sketches
Vaughan Williams A Sea Symphony (Symphony No. 1)
PROM 16 • 27 JULY

Debussy La mer
PROM 52 • 26 AUGUST

Britten Four Sea Interludes from 'Peter Grimes'
PROM 67 • 6 SEPTEMBER

The Proms on Radio, TV and Online

> **" I can see no better achievement of British culture to transmit to the world than the Proms, a festival that in its variety and spirit of communal love for music never ceases to exhilarate.**

Iranian-born harpsichordist Mahan Esfahani in 2012, the year he directed his own instrumental arrangement of Bach's *The Art of Fugue* at the Proms

When the BBC took over the Proms in 1927, the Corporation was just five years old. By broadcasting Proms concerts on the radio, it was fulfilling its remit to 'inform, educate and entertain', while the festival's own aim – to bring world-class orchestral music to audiences from all backgrounds and musical experiences – was extended on a national scale. By celebrating the BBC's centenary, the Proms also acknowledges a partnership that continues to bring world-class music to listeners around the globe.

On Radio

Hear every Prom live on BBC Radio 3 and on the BBC Sounds app, where you can listen on demand until 10 October. BBC Sounds offers all of BBC radio, music and podcasts, including every Prom live and on demand, so you can download and listen anytime, anywhere. Proms artists will also feature on Radio 3's *In Tune* every weekday evening throughout the season, with live performances and conversation.

On TV

Suzy Klein, Head of Commissioning for BBC Music TV, says: 'In the BBC's centenary year, we're so proud to be able to continue Henry Wood's vision of bringing the best of classical music to as many people as possible. For many, an annual "visit" to the Royal Albert Hall – via TV – is one of the highlights of the cultural year, and we are delighted to bring audiences 20 televised Proms, showcasing great home-grown orchestras and leading global ensembles, with a broadcast on BBC Four every Friday and Sunday evening during the season. We are thrilled to bring cameras back to the first full season since 2019, and to celebrate a glorious summer of music.'

Online

Make sure you visit bbc.co.uk/proms for everything you need to know about the Proms, including what's on, how to buy tickets, an A–Z of past performances and full details on how to watch and listen. ●

𝕏 @bbcproms f @theproms ⬡ @bbc_proms #bbcproms

BBC SOUNDS   **BBC iPLAYER**

THIS IS OUR
B B C

MAHLER
5 Scherzo
on Radio 3

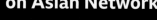
"NA NA"
on Asian Network

champagne supernova
on Radio 2

bbc.co.uk/100

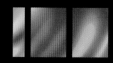
**100 YEARS
OF OUR BBC**

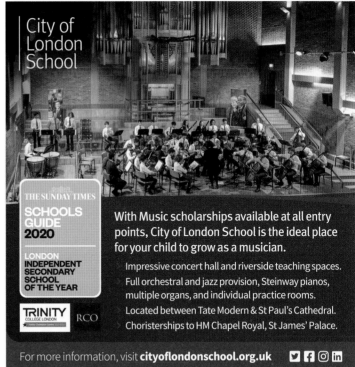

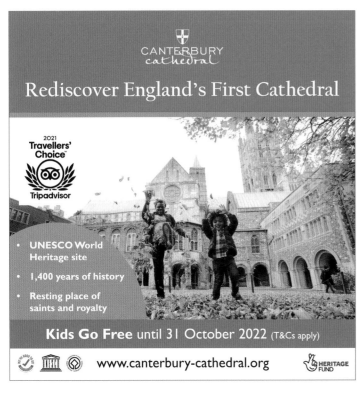

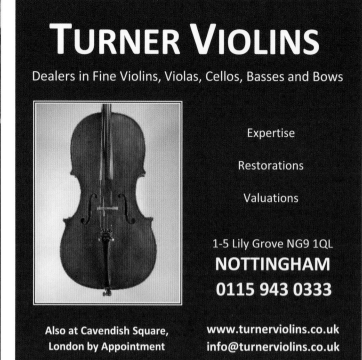

EVERY PROM LIVE

ON BBC RADIO 3

Then continue enjoying live performances all year round with *Radio 3 in Concert*, weeknights at 7.30pm

LISTEN ON
SOUNDS

Concert Listings

Full details of all the 2022 BBC Proms concerts – including 'Proms at' events around the UK – are listed in these pages, as well as Spotlight interviews with 25 artists.

For an at-a-glance calendar of the whole season, see inside front cover.

Please note: concert start-times vary – check before you book.

We hope you enjoy a summer of world-class music-making.

On Radio, TV and Online

 Every Prom is broadcast live on BBC Radio 3 and available on BBC Sounds until 10 October

 20 Proms are broadcast on BBC TV and available on BBC iPlayer until 10 October

Booking

Online
bbc.co.uk/promstickets
or royalalberthall.com

By phone
on 020 7070 4441[†]

General booking
opens at 9.00am on Saturday 21 May.
For booking, venue and access
information, see pages 153–161.

PROGRAMME CHANGES
Concert details were correct at the time of going to press. Please check the BBC Proms website for the latest information. The BBC reserves the right to alter artists or programmes as necessary.

† CALL COSTS
Standard geographic charges from landlines and mobiles apply. All calls may be recorded and monitored for training and quality-control purposes.

Spotlight on

Masabane Cecilia Rangwanasha
Prom 1

It's been quite a year for South African soprano Masabane Cecilia Rangwanasha, one that began last summer when she won the Song Prize at the BBC Cardiff Singer of the World competition. 'It opened up a lot of opportunities, and I had so many lovely messages on social media,' she explains. Covid restrictions meant no live audience, though her performance reached a huge number of people on TV and online: 'When you're used to communicating with live listeners, performing for the camera becomes something quite different!'

Rangwanasha is currently a member of the opera ensemble at the Bern Theatre, where she draws on the experience she gained as a Jette Parker Young Artist at the Royal Opera, Covent Garden. 'I owe the Royal Opera my career,' she says. 'Because of the pandemic there weren't so many live productions during my time there, but we did a lot online, which meant that my family in South Africa were able to watch too.'

Just a year after her Cardiff win, Rangwanasha makes her BBC Proms debut at the First Night in a work she feels closely connected to. 'Verdi's *Requiem* is very close to my heart. It's effectively a full opera, and he wrote the solo soprano part very well. I think it has a message for our current times, too: of being close together again, and of teaching us acceptance. We all have different beliefs, but they can bring so much strength to your life. For me, this is music that brings me closer to God.'

Friday 15 July

PROM 1
7.30pm–*c*9.00pm • Royal Albert Hall

● £14–£62 *(plus booking fee')*

FREDDIE DE TOMMASO

First Night of the Proms 2022

Verdi Requiem   84'

Masabane Cecilia Rangwanasha *soprano*
Jennifer Johnston *mezzo-soprano*
Freddie De Tommaso *tenor*
Kihwan Sim *bass-baritone*

BBC Symphony Chorus
Crouch End Festival Chorus
BBC Symphony Orchestra
Sakari Oramo *conductor*

There will be no interval

Hope and grief, mourning and celebration, thunder and tenderness come together in Verdi's mighty *Requiem*. After two years of reduced-sized performances, the Royal Albert Hall once again rings with the massed voices of the BBC Symphony Chorus and Crouch End Festival Chorus, launching the 2022 Proms with this choral masterpiece, which brings all the high drama of 19th-century opera to its emotive setting of the Latin Mass for the Dead. The BBC SO and Chief Conductor Sakari Oramo are joined by a starry team of young soloists that includes BBC Cardiff Singer of the World prize-winning soprano Masabane Cecilia Rangwanasha and rising British-Italian tenor Freddie De Tommaso.

🖥 *Broadcast on BBC TV tonight*

Saturday 16 July

PROM 2
6.30pm–*c*8.50pm • Royal Albert Hall

● £14–£62 *(plus booking fee')*

JOHN WILSON

Vaughan Williams Fantasia
on a Theme by Thomas Tallis   15'
Huw Watkins Flute Concerto   19'
Bax Tintagel   14'

INTERVAL

Walton Partita for Orchestra   15'
Elgar 'Enigma' Variations   29'

Adam Walker *flute*

Sinfonia of London
John Wilson *conductor*

Its Proms debut last year was hailed as 'astonishing', and praised for its 'revelatory' music-making. Now the award-winning Sinfonia of London and its conductor, Proms favourite John Wilson, return with a concert of English music. Bookending the programme are two beloved classics: Vaughan Williams's luminous *Fantasia on a Theme by Thomas Tallis* takes inspiration from Tudor choral music, while Elgar immortalised friends and family in the affectionate character sketches of his 'Enigma' Variations. The Arthurian castle of Tintagel is glimpsed from Cornish cliffs in Bax's tone-poem, while Walton's virtuosic *Partita for Orchestra* draws on the Mediterranean landscapes the composer knew so well. Adam Walker is soloist in the Flute Concerto that Huw Watkins wrote with his 'amazing sound' in mind. *See 'The Shape of British Music', pages 44–49.*

🖥 *Recorded for broadcast on BBC Four on Sunday 17 July*

Saturday 16 July

10.30pm–c11.30pm • Royal Albert Hall

⬤ £10–£35 *(plus booking fee*)*

SIAN ELERI

Radio 1 Relax at the Proms

Celebrating the BBC's centenary year, the Proms partners with Radio 1 Relax for a late-night wind-down. Relax with *Radio 1's Chillest Show* presenter Sian Eleri, who appears onstage to introduce a stripped-back set of collaborations and explorations.

📻 *Recorded for future broadcast on Radio 1 Relax (BBC Sounds)*

🖥 *Broadcast on BBC Four on Friday 22 July*

Sunday 17 July

PROM 4

7.30pm–c9.30pm • Royal Albert Hall

⬤ £18–£72 *(plus booking fee*)*

CYNTHIA ERIVO

Cynthia Erivo: Legendary Voices

Cynthia Erivo

BBC Concert Orchestra
Edwin Outwater *conductor*

With Tony, Grammy and Emmy awards to her name, British actress, singer, songwriter and producer Cynthia Erivo is a creative powerhouse. Her career has taken her from West End to Broadway, theatre to film, stage to recording studio. Now she makes her BBC Proms debut, backed by the BBC Concert Orchestra, in a performance celebrating legendary singers such as Nina Simone, Shirley Bassey, Billie Holiday and Gladys Knight.

🖥 *Recorded for broadcast on BBC Two*

Spotlight on
Adam Walker • Prom 2

'My first-ever memory of a live classical concert is watching the Proms on TV as a child. I think the fact that I was more animated watching a Prom than watching *ChuckleVision* was a sign to my parents!' Nottinghamshire-born Adam Walker – for several years Principal Flute with the London Symphony Orchestra and now a soloist in demand worldwide – is talking about the formative role the Proms played in his early music-making. 'My first time playing at the festival,' he continues, 'was as a 14-year-old in Mahler's Eighth with the National Youth Orchestra of Great Britain and Sir Simon Rattle. It was a huge occasion. I still remember it very clearly.'

For his Prom on 16 July Walker brings the 2013 Flute Concerto written for him by Welsh-born Huw Watkins. 'I first met Huw in 2010: I played with him at the Gregynog Festival, and that resulted in a long-lasting performance partnership.' Following the brief *Capriccio* that Watkins wrote for their Gregynog performance, Walker asked him for a larger concerto. 'Huw understands the innate aspects of flute playing, as well as my own particular sound and quirks. He's very familiar with my playing from our duo work, and he wrote with my sound in mind.' How much input did Walker have in the writing of the piece? 'Very little, actually. I didn't want to get in the way of Huw's creative process. He wrote the piece, we met and played it through at the piano, and I was an extremely happy flute player!'

Every Prom live on BBC Radio 3 and available on BBC Sounds

20 Proms on BBC TV and available on BBC iPlayer

Monday 18 July

PROMS AT BELFAST ☀
1.00pm–*c*2.00pm • Waterfront Hall, Studio

For ticket prices, see bbc.co.uk/promstickets

HEBRIDES ENSEMBLE

Xenakis
Allegro molto   1'
Akea   14'

Messiaen Pièce pour piano et
quatuor à cordes   4'

Xenakis Ittidra   9'

Ravel Pavane pour une infante
défunte   6'

Xenakis À r. (Hommage à Ravel)   3'

Messiaen Quartet for the End
of Time – Louange à l'Immortalité
de Jésus   9'

Hebrides Ensemble

Scottish chamber collective the Hebrides
Ensemble celebrates the 100th anniversary of
revolutionary composer Iannis Xenakis, who
combined music and mathematical models
to create 'alien' sounds of 'wild beauty'. A
Greek-born naturalised Frenchman and pupil
of Messiaen, Xenakis was steeped in the French
tradition. His homage to Ravel, *À r.*, nods to his
predecessor's liquid piano-writing, while his
strident *Akea* contrasts with the violin-and-
piano movement from Messiaen's *Quartet
for the End of Time*, a mesmerising glimpse
into eternity. The concert also features the
intricately layered sounds of the string sextet
Ittidra and Ravel's elegant, much-loved *Pavane*.
See 'Sound by Design', pages 64–67.

Monday 18 July

PROM 5
7.30pm–*c*9.40pm • Royal Albert Hall

⏺ £8.50–£42 *(plus booking fee')*

LAWRENCE POWER

Bach, orch. Webern
Musical Offering – Ricercar a 6   8'

Cassandra Miller
Viola Concerto   *c*25'
BBC co-commission: world premiere

INTERVAL

Bruckner Symphony No. 6
in A major   54'

Lawrence Power *viola*

BBC Philharmonic
Omer Meir Wellber *conductor*

This season the Proms looks beyond the
piano and violin to concertos that explore
more unusual instruments, including the
tuba, trombone and theremin. Award-winning
violist Lawrence Power launches the strand
with a new concerto by Canadian composer
Cassandra Miller. It is the latest in a long series
of major works Power has commissioned for
an instrument whose range and reputation he
continues to expand. The concert opens with
Webern's airy, pellucid arrangement of Bach's
'richest piece of fugal writing' – the six-part
Ricercar from his *Musical Offering* – and closes
with the symphony Bruckner himself considered
his 'sassiest'. Baffling the composer's
contemporaries with its relative brevity and
sudden shifts of musical direction, it has been
praised for its 'exceptionally beautiful' themes
and the subtlety of its instrumentation.
See 'Sounds Electric', pages 92–94.

Tuesday 19 July

PROM 6
7.00pm–*c*8.35pm • Royal Albert Hall

⏺ £8.50–£42 *(plus booking fee')*

OMER MEIR WELLBER

Vaughan Williams
Symphony No. 4 in F minor   30'

INTERVAL

Tippett Symphony No. 4   33'

BBC Philharmonic
Omer Meir Wellber *conductor*

Celebrations of Vaughan Williams's 150th
anniversary run right through this season.
The composer who defined British music for
a generation, and whose legacy continued
to shape it, may still be best known for the
pastoral beauty of *The Lark Ascending (see Prom
52)* but his music is startling for its breadth. The
ferocity of the composer's Fourth Symphony –
described by Walton as 'the greatest since
Beethoven' – showcases the raw power of the
orchestra. The BBC Philharmonic and Chief
Conductor Omer Meir Wellber pair it with
Tippett's Fourth Symphony, an arresting work
that takes listeners from the first breath to the
final gasp of human life. *See 'The Shape of British
Music', pages 44–49.*

**Every Prom live
on BBC Radio 3
and available on
BBC Sounds**

Tuesday 19 July

PROM 7 • LATE NIGHT 🌙

10.15pm–c11.20pm • Royal Albert Hall

● £10–£35 (plus booking fee')

ALICE COOTE

Purcell Dido and Aeneas   55'
(concert performance)

Alice Coote Dido
James Newby Aeneas
Gemma Summerfield Belinda
Madeleine Shaw Sorceress
Nardus Williams Second Woman
Nicky Spence Sailor
Tim Mead Spirit

La Nuova Musica Choir
La Nuova Musica
David Bates harpsichord/conductor

There will be no interval

Abandoned by her lover, Dido must choose
between death or a life without love. Her painful
decision is powerfully dramatised in some of
the most emotive music of the Baroque period,
including Dido's famous lament, 'When I am laid
in earth'. Period-instrument ensemble La Nuova
Musica makes its Proms debut under Artistic
Director David Bates, who made his own Proms
debut last year conducting Mozart's *Requiem*.
They are joined by an exciting cast led by
leading mezzo-soprano Alice Coote and former
Kathleen Ferrier Prize-winner James Newby in
the title-roles. *See 'The Opera Doctor Will See
You Now', pages 54–55.*

Wednesday 20 July

PROM 8

7.30pm–c9.30pm • Royal Albert Hall

● £9.50–£52 (plus booking fee')

DALIA STASEVSKA

Jóhannsson The Miners' Hymns –
They Being Dead Yet Speaketh   10'
Rachmaninov Piano Concerto No. 2
in C minor   35'

INTERVAL

Hildur Guðnadóttir new work   c15'
BBC commission: world premiere

Tchaikovsky Fantasy-Overture
'Romeo and Juliet'   19'

Alexander Gavrylyuk piano

BBC Singers
BBC Symphony Orchestra
Dalia Stasevska conductor

The worlds of classical and film music come
together in this concert by the BBC SO and
Principal Guest Conductor Dalia Stasevska.
Rachmaninov's passionate Piano Concerto
No. 2 may have been written for the concert
hall, but it had a successful second life
on screen in films including *Brief Encounter* and
The Seven Year Itch. It is performed along with
a mesmeric excerpt from Golden Globe-winner
Jóhann Jóhannsson's score for *The Miners'
Hymns*, Tchaikovsky's cinematic, Shakespeare-
inspired *Romeo and Juliet* overture and a world
premiere from Oscar-winning *Joker* composer
Hildur Guðnadóttir. *See 'Mood Music',
pages 72–77.*

Spotlight on
Lawrence Power • Prom 5

'An increasingly large part of my life now is
spent working with composers and playing
new music. I love it: there's no expectation,
no tradition when you're premiering a new
piece. It's the purest thing you can do as
a musician, and when you return to playing
older music, you realise that most of the
conventions that have grown up around
it are irrelevant.' Viola player Lawrence
Power is considering the cleansing effects
of being the very first performer to tackle
an entirely new piece of music – something
he did with his series of 10 filmed Lockdown
Commissions in 2020, and something he's
continuing with his Viola Commissioning
Circle, which aims to bring 10 new viola
concertos into being across 10 years.

Power has already given the first
performances of concertos by Gerald
Barry and Anders Hillborg as part of
the project. The next, by Canadian-born
composer Cassandra Miller, he premieres
at the Proms on 18 July. 'I'm super-excited
because Cassandra is a unique voice in
music today. She also likes performers to
bring their own ideas to the table, which is
not always the case with composers.' He's
reluctant to give much more away at this
stage, however. 'The foundation of the
piece is a really interesting idea, which I'm
sure will become clear in the finished score.
But Cassandra is also a composer who
can surprise you. She has a great dramatic
ear for music, which will really come into
its own in the intense arena of the Hall.'

Thursday 21 July

PROM 9
7.00pm–*c*9.05pm • Royal Albert Hall

🔵 £8.50–£42 *(plus booking fee')*

ARIANE MATIAKH

Ravel Shéhérazade – ouverture de féerie   16'

Sally Beamish Hive   *c*23'
BBC co-commission: world premiere

INTERVAL

Rimsky-Korsakov Scheherazade 42'

Catrin Finch *harp*

BBC National Orchestra of Wales
Ariane Matiakh *conductor*

The legend of Scheherazade and her bewitching stories from *One Thousand and One Nights* are vividly captured in both Rimsky-Korsakov's orchestral suite – a dazzling musical portrait of the East, full of shipwrecks, love scenes and crowded bazaars – and Ravel's sensually beautiful overture, written for a never-completed opera. We're in more familiar landscapes in Sally Beamish's *Hive*, which traces the life of a beehive across four seasons, starting with the gentle stir and shimmer of winter and climaxing in the swarms, dances and battles of summer. Award-winning Welsh harpist Catrin Finch is the soloist in this world-premiere performance. *See 'Mood Music', pages 72–77.*

Friday 22 July

PROM 10
7.30pm–*c*9.40pm • Royal Albert Hall

🔵 £9.50–£52 *(plus booking fee')*

BRAMWELL TOVEY

Music for Royal Occasions

Programme to include:

Handel Coronation Anthem 'Zadok the Priest'; Water Music – excerpts 20'

Walton Coronation March 'Orb and Sceptre'   7'

Britten Courtly Dances from 'Gloriana'   9'

Parry Coronation Anthem 'I was glad' 8'

Judith Weir I love all beauteous things   4'

Vaughan Williams Silence and Music   5'

Elgar Pomp and Circumstance March No. 4 in G major   4'

and works by Byrd and Ireland, as well as a new commission by Cheryl Frances-Hoad

BBC Singers
BBC Concert Orchestra
Bramwell Tovey *conductor*

There will be one interval

Whether it's choral anthems, grand marches or jubilant dances, music has a long and fruitful relationship with monarchy. The Proms celebrates the Queen's Platinum Jubilee year with a concert featuring music inspired by royal occasions reaching back to Elizabeth I. *See 'Music & the Monarchy', pages 40–43.*

📺 *Broadcast on BBC TV on Sunday 24 July*

Saturday 23 July

PROMS 11 & 12 ☀
11.00am–*c*12.00pm &
3.00pm–*c*4.00pm • Royal Albert Hall

🔵 £8.50–£20 *(plus booking fee')*

JOJO & GRAN GRAN

CBeebies Prom: A Journey into the Ocean

Nigel Clarke *(from 'The Baby Club')*
Rory Crawford *(from 'Teeny Tiny Creatures')*
Andy Day *(from 'Andy's Adventures')*
Chantelle Lindsay *(from 'Teeny Tiny Creatures')*
Maddie Moate *(from 'Do You Know?')*
Puja Panchkoty *(from 'Andy's Adventures')*

Southbank Sinfonia
Kwamé Ryan *conductor*

There will be no interval

AD *11.00am performance audio-described by Timna Fibert*
BSL *British Sign Language-interpreted by Angie Newman*
R *Relaxed performances with large screens*

Join your CBeebies friends on an underwater family adventure. As you travel the musical world, you'll find endangered creatures while collecting sounds and photos with JoJo & Gran Gran for an ocean-themed scrapbook. *See 'Behold … The Sea!', pages 104–107.*

BBC Proms relaxed performances are designed to suit individuals or groups who feel more comfortable attending concerts in a relaxed environment. There is a relaxed attitude to noise and audience-members are free to leave and re-enter the auditorium at any point. There will be chill-out areas, where spaces are made for anyone needing a bit of quiet time before or during the performance. For full details, visit bbc.co.uk/proms.

📻 *Broadcast live on BBC Radio 3 (Prom 12)*

📺 *Recorded for future broadcast on CBeebies*

Saturday 23 July

PROMS AT SAGE GATESHEAD
7.30pm–c9.30pm • Sage Gateshead

For ticket prices, see bbc.co.uk/promstickets

DINIS SOUSA

Folk Connections

John Adams Shaker Loops   26'

Folk music and Spell Songs   c25'

INTERVAL

Dvořák Symphony No. 9 in E minor, 'From the New World'   40'

Voices of the River's Edge
Spell Songs
Royal Northern Sinfonia
Dinis Sousa *conductor*

Dvořák's most popular symphony, 'From the New World', was inspired by African American and Native American tunes. Another slice of American musical identity comes with John Adams's hypnotic *Shaker Loops*, whose rapid repetitions brought to the composer's mind the ecstatic trembling dances of a New England Shaker colony. Karine Polwart, Rachel Newton and Jim Molyneux from the folk ensemble Spell Songs return to the Proms following their appearance at The Lost Words Prom in 2019, drawing on folk music from both America and the British Isles. Joining them are the specially formed Voices of the River's Edge, showcasing young singers aged 16 to 30 from around the North East of England. Sage Gateshead's resident orchestra, the Royal Northern Sinfonia, appears with its new Principal Conductor, Dinis Sousa.

Sunday 24 July

PROM 13
6.30pm–c10.20pm • Royal Albert Hall

● **£14–£62** *(plus booking fee')*

MARTA FONTANALS-SIMMONS

Smyth The Wreckers   170'
(semi-staged; sung in French, with English surtitles)

Cast to include:

Markus Brück *Pascoe*
James Rutherford *Lawrence*
Rodrigo Porras Garulo *Mark*
Lauren Fagan *Avis*
Donovan Singletary *Harvey*
Jeffrey Lloyd-Roberts *Tallan*
Marta Fontanals-Simmons *Jack*

Glyndebourne Festival Opera
London Philharmonic Orchestra
Robin Ticciati *conductor*

There will be two intervals

Admired by Mahler and Britten and praised as a 'masterpiece' by Thomas Beecham, Ethel Smyth's opera *The Wreckers* – a psychological drama of 'wrecking, religion and love' – was the pinnacle of the composer's career. With its sweeping musical soundscapes, passionate central love story and radical interrogation of fear, hypocrisy and mob violence, it's a compelling piece of music-theatre, whose heroine is a mirror of her fascinating, unorthodox creator. Glyndebourne presents the opera for the first time with its original score and French libretto. Robin Ticciati conducts an exciting international cast in this semi-staged performance. *See 'The Shape of British Music', pages 44–49; 'The Opera Doctor Will See You Now', pages 54–55; 'Behold … The Sea!', pages 104–107.*

Spotlight on
Robin Ticciati • Prom 13

Robin Ticciati is no stranger to the Proms, having brought several Glyndebourne opera productions – from *The Marriage of Figaro* to *Tristan and Isolde* – to the Royal Albert Hall in recent years. But it's a far less familiar opera he conducts this year: *The Wreckers* by Ethel Smyth. 'Sadly, it's been largely neglected,' he says, 'despite being admired by Mahler, Bruno Walter, Thomas Beecham and others. It didn't help that Smyth's original score was never fully realised. She was so upset by how the Leipzig premiere went that she stormed into the pit and retrieved the music. Glyndebourne has been burrowing down in the British Library to uncover Smyth's original vision. Once people hear it in this new edition, perhaps then we can judge its place in the operatic canon.'

It's clearly an opera that Ticciati himself admires. 'She doesn't hold back for one moment! The music comes straight from her heart. It's an explosion of colour and extravagance that always serves the drama. And, though Smyth's opulence draws upon her many influences, her compositional voice feels unique and, more importantly, honest to herself.' So what are the musical challenges of transferring a fully staged production to a concert venue? 'My big one is balance. We'll have worked towards the perfect mixture between voice and pit at Glyndebourne, and then for one evening everything has to be adjusted!'

Spotlight on

Kazuki Yamada • Prom 14

Japanese conductor Kazuki Yamada becomes the City of Birmingham Symphony Orchestra's Chief Conductor in spring 2023, but the pair already have a decade-long relationship. 'I first conducted the CBSO in 2012, then again in 2014. In 2016 we spent two weeks together while on tour in Japan and I got to know almost every musician.' He's also been Principal Guest Conductor since 2018. 'I think the players have some kind of telepathy,' he explains. 'My English isn't so great yet, but there are no problems communicating. I feel very comfortable working with them.'

Yamada makes his Proms debut on 25 July with what he might almost consider his 'lucky' piece of music. 'Rachmaninov's Second Symphony means so much to me, and it's marked some important moments in my life. I made my UK debut with it, conducting the BBC Symphony Orchestra at the Barbican in 2011, and I conducted it for my debut with Rome's Orchestra dell'Accademia Nazionale di Santa Cecilia, and with several Japanese orchestras too.'

Less familiar is Ethel Smyth's Concerto for Violin and Horn, which shares the billing. 'To be honest, I didn't know Smyth at all before discussing the concert. But, when I listened to a recording, I was surprised at how great the music is – I actually ended up feeling ashamed I didn't know it already. It's deeply Romantic music, but with new elements as well – just the kind of music I love conducting with the CBSO.'

Monday 25 July

📍 PROMS AT **TRURO** ☀
1.00pm–c2.00pm • Hall for Cornwall

For ticket prices, see bbc.co.uk/promstickets

ALIM BEISEMBAYEV

D. Scarlatti
Piano Sonata in G major, K13   3'
Piano Sonata in C sharp minor, K247   4'
Piano Sonata in C minor, K22   3'

Liszt Transcendental Études – Nos. 3–5   15'

Chopin Piano Sonata No. 2 in B flat minor, Op. 35   23'

Alim Beisembayev *piano*

There will be no interval

Following his First Prize and Audience Prize wins at the 2021 Leeds International Piano Competition, where he was praised for his 'polish' and 'maturity', dynamic young Kazakh pianist Alim Beisembayev makes his Proms debut. At the centre of the programme is Chopin's enigmatic Sonata No. 2, with its haunting Funeral March. This darkness collides with the dangerous brilliance of Liszt's *Transcendental Études* – to the piano what Paganini's *Caprices* are to the violin – and three contrasting sonatas by Domenico Scarlatti, including the joyful G major Sonata, K13, and the solemn C sharp minor Sonata, K247.

Monday 25 July

PROM 14
7.30pm–c9.40pm • Royal Albert Hall

● £9.50–£52 *(plus booking fee¹)*

ELENA URIOSTE

Glinka Ruslan and Lyudmila – overture   5'

Smyth Concerto for Violin and Horn   27'

INTERVAL

Rachmaninov Symphony No. 2 in E minor   60'

Elena Urioste *violin*
Ben Goldscheider *horn*

City of Birmingham Symphony Orchestra
Kazuki Yamada *conductor*

The City of Birmingham Symphony Orchestra makes its first Proms appearance under Chief Conductor Designate Kazuki Yamada with one of the great Romantic symphonies. Charged with nostalgic yearning, swelling through the gorgeous slow movement and bursting out in an ecstatic finale, Rachmaninov's Symphony No. 2 finds echo in the late-Romantic warmth and full-bodied lyricism of Ethel Smyth's Concerto for Violin and Horn, dedicated to Proms founder-conductor Henry Wood. Two rising stars – violinist Elena Urioste and horn player Ben Goldscheider – are the soloists in a virtuosic work whose composer is finally reclaiming her place as one of the leading British voices of her generation. The concert opens with the vivacious overture from Glinka's Pushkin-inspired opera *Ruslan and Lyudmila*. *See 'The Shape of British Music', pages 44–49.*

Tuesday 26 July

PROM 15
7.30pm–c9.40pm • Royal Albert Hall

⬤ **£8.50–£42** (plus booking fee*)

JOHAN DALENE

Bernstein Candide – overture   5'
Walker Variations for Orchestra   14'
Barber Violin Concerto   23'
INTERVAL
Tchaikovsky Symphony No. 4
in F minor   44'

Johan Dalene violin

BBC Symphony Orchestra
Jordan de Souza conductor

From the explosive energy of Bernstein's
Candide overture to the heart-tugging pathos
of Tchaikovsky's Symphony No. 4, rising-star
Canadian conductor Jordan de Souza makes
his Proms debut with a programme that runs
the gamut of human experience and emotion.
Young Swedish violinist Johan Dalene (currently
a BBC Radio 3 New Generation Artist) is the
soloist in Barber's Violin Concerto – its long-
breathed lyricism a foil to the charged concision
of centenary composer George Walker's
Variations for Orchestra. At the climax of the
programme is Tchaikovsky's deeply personal
Fourth Symphony, a musical exploration of the
'inexorable power' of fate. See 'A World of Music',
pages 36–38.

Wednesday 27 July

PROM 16
7.00pm–c9.10pm • Royal Albert Hall

⬤ **£9.50–£52** (plus booking fee*)

ELIZABETH LLEWELLYN

Carwithen Bishop Rock   8'
G. Williams Sea Sketches   19'
INTERVAL
Vaughan Williams A Sea
Symphony (Symphony No. 1)   67'

Elizabeth Llewellyn soprano
Andrew Foster-Williams bass-baritone

BBC Symphony Chorus
BBC National Chorus of Wales
BBC National Orchestra of Wales
Andrew Manze conductor

'Behold, the sea itself …' Home to Sirens and
storms, crashing waves and calming swells,
the sea is at the centre of this atmospheric
programme from Andrew Manze, the BBC
National Orchestra of Wales and joint BBC
choruses. Vaughan Williams's expansive A Sea
Symphony, with its arresting choral opening, is
prefaced by sea pictures from two neglected
20th-century women composers now enjoying
a revival. There's a filmic energy and vividness
to Doreen Carwithen's Bishop Rock overture,
while Grace Williams's Sea Sketches, inspired by
her family home on the Welsh coast, captures
the sea's vivacity and mercurial mood swings.
See 'The Shape of British Music', pages 44–49;
'Behold … The Sea!', pages 104–107.

🖥 Broadcast on BBC Four on Friday 29 July

Spotlight on
Jordan de Souza • Prom 15

Toronto-born Jordan de Souza made
his conducting debut aged 20 and, just 14
years later, he's already a well-established
figure in opera houses worldwide. 'Opera
is an intensely collaborative art form that's
eternally unpredictable – the potential for
disaster lurks at every corner!' he says.
'But it's a unique pleasure to sit right in
the middle of it and guide the action.'

One of the well-received Berlin
productions that Souza conducted was
Bernstein's Candide, whose overture opens
his Proms debut on 26 July. Bernstein is
clearly someone Souza greatly admires: 'He
belongs to that rarefied group of musicians
who were excellent conductors *and*
composers, which means they knew how
to thrill musicians and audiences alike.'
Closing the Prom is the Fourth Symphony
by another of Souza's favourites: 'I adore
Tchaikovsky's music. He understood
the power of a great musical idea, and
the emotions he taps into are on such
an archetypal level that we inevitably
recognise our own stories in his music.'

Away from the concert hall, Souza
isn't averse to entertaining his Twitter
followers with witty birthday tributes
to the great composers, seemingly
improvised at the piano. 'Believe it or
not, those are like little musical sudokus!
I work them out carefully: my goal is to
play the piece as the composer intended,
but also to sneak in some cheeky 'Happy
Birthday' quotes in unexpected ways.'

Thursday 28 July

PROM 17

7.30pm–c9.45pm • Royal Albert Hall

🔘 £8.50–£42 *(plus booking fee*)*

JENNIFER WALSHE

Jennifer Walshe The Site of an Investigation   *33'*

London premiere

INTERVAL

Brahms A German Requiem   *68'*

Jennifer Walshe *voice*
Elena Tsallagova *soprano*
Shenyang *bass-baritone*

National Youth Choir of Great Britain
BBC Scottish Symphony Orchestra
Ilan Volkov *conductor*

Brahms's *A German Requiem* is a work as much of consolation as of loss. A profoundly personal response to a universal public ritual, it tempers doubt with hope in some of Brahms's loveliest and most deeply felt music. Where Brahms reinvents the Requiem for his own age, Jennifer Walshe turns her attention to the symphony, deconstructing and reassembling it into the funny, dramatic, irrepressibly eclectic *The Site of an Investigation* – a musical reflection of 'the psychedelia of everyday life'.

Friday 29 July

PROM 18

7.30pm–c9.30pm • Royal Albert Hall

🔘 £9.50–£52 *(plus booking fee*)*

COLIN CURRIE

Bruckner, arr. Skrowaczewski
String Quintet in F major – Adagio   *16'*
Nicole Lizée Blurr Is the Colour of My True Love's Eyes   *25'*

BBC co-commission: European premiere

INTERVAL

Shostakovich Symphony No. 5 in D minor   *44'*

Colin Currie *percussion*

BBC Scottish Symphony Orchestra
Alpesh Chauhan *conductor*

Like the slow movements of his towering symphonies, the richly passionate Adagio from Bruckner's String Quintet – his only mature piece of chamber music – shimmers with a mystical quality. It finds a counterpart in the deeply poignant slow movement of Shostakovich's Fifth Symphony – with which the composer managed to appease the Soviet censors while also expressing the horrors of his time. This contrasts with the more joyful rhythms of Canadian composer Nicole Lizée's new percussion concerto. Award-winning percussionist Colin Currie is the soloist in the European premiere of a work written specially for him.

Saturday 30 July

📍 PROMS AT **BATTERSEA**   ☀

4.00pm–c5.00pm • Battersea Arts Centre

ALICE FARNHAM

BBC Young Composer

BBC Concert Orchestra
Alice Farnham *conductor*

There will be no interval

A showcase of new commissions specially written by recent winners of the BBC Young Composer competition. Be first to hear pieces by composing talents of the future: Chelsea Becker, Isaac Bristow, Maddy Chassar-Hesketh, Will Everitt, Theo Kendall, Daniel Liu and Jenna Stewart.

Every Prom live on BBC Radio 3 and available on BBC Sounds

Saturday 30 July

PROM 19
7.30pm–c9.30pm • Royal Albert Hall

● £14–£62 *(plus booking fee')*

SIR MARK ELDER

Dukas The Sorcerer's Apprentice   *12'*
Respighi Fountains of Rome   *17'*

INTERVAL

Puccini Il tabarro   *55'*
(concert performance; sung in Italian, with English surtitles)

George Gagnidze *Michele*
Natalya Romaniw *Giorgetta*
Ivan Gyngazov *Luigi*
Daniela Barcellona *La Frugola*
Alasdair Elliott *'Tinca'*
Simon Shibambu *'Talpa'*
Jung Soo Yun *Ballad-Seller*

RCM Opera Chorus
Hallé
Sir Mark Elder *conductor*

Sir Mark Elder and the Hallé bring Puccini's atmospheric Parisian tragedy *Il tabarro* to the Proms – a score that swirls and throbs with the energy of the River Seine. Natalya Romaniw stars as the unhappily married Giorgetta, whose affair is the catalyst for murder. Two orchestral favourites set the watery scene: Respighi's *Fountains of Rome* – by turns glistening in the sunlight and swathed in dawn mist – and the irrepressible musical antics of Dukas's *The Sorcerer's Apprentice. See 'The Opera Doctor Will See You Now', pages 54–55.*

🖵 *Broadcast on BBC Four on Sunday 31 July*

Sunday 31 July

PROM 20
7.30pm–c9.30pm • Royal Albert Hall

● £9.50–£52 *(plus booking fee')*

TOM BORROW

Xenakis Jonchaies   *16'*
Ravel Piano Concerto in G major   *23'*

INTERVAL

Stravinsky The Rite of Spring   *33'*

Tom Borrow *piano*

BBC Symphony Orchestra
Martyn Brabbins *conductor*

Rites and rituals run through this concert given by Martyn Brabbins and the BBC SO. Scored for 109 musicians, centenary composer Xenakis's *Jonchaies* is a powerful hit of sound and sensation. Intricate mathematical patterns underpin a work of visceral sonic drama – a natural companion to the primal rhythms and hypnotic dances of Stravinsky's ballet *The Rite of Spring*, which reportedly prompted a riot at its Paris premiere in 1913. BBC Radio 3 New Generation Artist Tom Borrow is the soloist in Ravel's Piano Concerto in G major – its light-hearted, glittering brilliance a foil to so much intensity. *See 'Rolling with the Punches', pages 20–24; 'Sound by Design', pages 64–67.*

20 Proms on BBC TV and available on BBC iPlayer

Spotlight on
Natalya Romaniw • Prom 19

'I do love to sing Puccini!' Welsh-born soprano Natalya Romaniw is looking forward to her Proms performance in the Italian's tragic one-act opera *Il tabarro*. 'This will be my first time singing Giorgetta. I actually learnt the role during lockdown in the hope that the performance we'd planned for 2020 might go ahead. Like most of Puccini's women, Giorgetta thinks with her heart rather than her head. She's lost a child and feels trapped in a mundane, repetitive life – although whether the romance she begins is more than just lust remains to be seen for me …'

It's a concert performance that Romaniw is so eagerly anticipating. How does she find singing opera in a concert hall? 'It's always a question of becoming the character. We're used to costumes, wigs and make-up to transform us into someone else. A concert performance can sometimes feel very exposed. That said, it gives performers and audience an immediacy and focus you don't get when you're running around onstage.'

She's looking forward, too, to performing again with conductor Sir Mark Elder. 'I was quite scared the first time I worked with him and I was hoping to impress. It was Beethoven's Ninth, and three of us soloists were late onstage because we hadn't heard the call to come down. Then we all got the giggles and nearly didn't make it at all! But Mark was lovely. We all went out for dinner after and, of course, he wasn't scary at all.'

Monday 1 August

📍 PROMS AT **BRISTOL** ☀

1.00pm–c2.00pm • St George's Bristol

For ticket prices, see bbc.co.uk/promstickets

ALINA IBRAGIMOVA & CÉDRIC TIBERGHIEN

Brian Legend   7'
Ysaÿe Poème élégiaque   15'
Franck Violin Sonata in A major   29'

Alina Ibragimova *violin*
Cédric Tiberghien *piano*

Romance runs through this recital of chamber music by violinist Alina Ibragimova and pianist Cédric Tiberghien. Franck's lyrical Violin Sonata, with its virtuosic piano-writing, was a wedding gift for violinist Eugène Ysaÿe – its performance here marks 200 years since the composer's birth. The rhapsodic music of Ysaÿe's own *Poème élégiaque* follows Romeo and Juliet from love to death and sombre funeral rites. The duo cross the Channel to mark another anniversary: 50 years since the death of Havergal Brian. The British composer may be best known for his vast 'Gothic' Symphony, but *Legend* (written at the same time) sees him at his most dramatically distilled.

Every Prom live on BBC Radio 3 and available on BBC Sounds

Monday 1 August

PROM 21

7.30pm–c9.00pm • Royal Albert Hall

⬤ £14–£62 *(plus booking fee*)*

ROBERT AMES

Gaming Prom: From 8-Bit to Infinity

Programme to include:

Hildur Guðnadóttir/Sam Slater,
arr. Robert Ames
Battlefield 2042 – suite   14'
European premiere

Jessica Curry Dear Esther – I Have Begun My Ascent   4'

and excerpts from:

Yoko Shimomura
Kingdom Hearts   4'
Kow Otani Shadow of the Colossus   8'

Royal Philharmonic Orchestra
Robert Ames *conductor*

There will be no interval

Like the film industry before it, gaming has inspired a whole wave of composers who have created new sound-worlds to match the medium's ever more richly imagined visual realms. Returning after his *Pioneers of Sound* and sci-fi film music Proms, Robert Ames conducts the Royal Philharmonic Orchestra for the first-ever Gaming Prom. The Royal Albert Hall is transformed into a vast sonic chamber in a mini history of gaming, from classic console titles of the 1980s to the latest release in the *Battlefield* franchise.

🖥 *Broadcast on BBC Four on Friday 5 August*

Tuesday 2 August

PROM 22

7.30pm–c9.45pm • Royal Albert Hall

⬤ £9.50–£52 *(plus booking fee*)*

PATRICIA KOPATCHINSKAJA

Xenakis O-Mega   4'
Shostakovich Violin Concerto
No. 1 in A minor   39'

INTERVAL

Tom Service and Nicholas Collon introduce Beethoven's Fifth Symphony   c15'
Beethoven Symphony No. 5 in C minor   31'

Patricia Kopatchinskaja *violin*
Tom Service *presenter*

Aurora Orchestra
Nicholas Collon *conductor/presenter*

Beethoven's Fifth Symphony has been played well over 100 times at the Proms – but you've never heard it like this. Conductor Nicholas Collon and presenter Tom Service are your guides, taking this much-loved work apart in front of your ears before the Aurora Orchesta performs the entire symphony from memory. In the first half the orchestra is joined by maverick violinist Patricia Kopatchinskaja, whose 'joyous' and 'compelling' performance of Bartók's Second Violin Concerto was a highlight last year. She performs Shostakovich's mercurial First Violin Concerto, whose demanding writing climaxes in a boisterous folk celebration. The concert opens with centenary composer Xenakis's final work, the solemn *O-Mega*. See 'Rolling with the Punches', pages 20–24; 'Sound by Design', pages 64–67.

Wednesday 3 August

PROM 23
11.00am–c11.55am • Royal Albert Hall

● £8.50–£20 (plus booking fee*)

NICHOLAS COLLON

Relaxed Prom

Tom Service and Nicholas Collon introduce Beethoven's Fifth Symphony *c15'*

Beethoven Symphony No. 5 in C minor *31'*

Tom Service *presenter*

Aurora Orchestra
Nicholas Collon *conductor/presenter*

There will be no interval

AD Audio-described by Timna Fibert
BSL British Sign Language-interpreted by Angie Newman
R Relaxed performances

You've never heard Beethoven's Fifth Symphony quite like this! The Aurora Orchestra, conductor Nicholas Collon and presenter Tom Service are your guides as they take apart this revolutionary symphony – with its famous four-note opening – revealing the many questions it raises, as well as a few answers, before performing the entire work from memory.

BBC Proms relaxed performances are designed to suit individuals or groups who feel more comfortable attending concerts in a relaxed environment. There is a relaxed attitude to noise and audience-members are free to leave and re-enter the auditorium at any point. There will be chill-out areas, where spaces are made for anyone needing a bit of quiet time before or during the performance. For full details, visit bbc.co.uk/proms.

Wednesday 3 August

PROM 24
7.00pm–c9.15pm • Royal Albert Hall

● £8.50–£42 (plus booking fee*)

MIAH PERSSON

Caroline Shaw Entr'acte *13'*
Mendelssohn Violin Concerto in E minor *26'*

INTERVAL

Mahler Symphony No. 4 in G major *54'*

Clara-Jumi Kang *violin*
Miah Persson *soprano*

BBC National Orchestra of Wales
Ryan Bancroft *conductor*

BBC NOW and Principal Conductor Ryan Bancroft venture through the musical looking-glass in a programme spanning almost 200 years. Pulitzer Prize-winning American composer Caroline Shaw's *Entr'acte* takes a Haydn string quartet as the starting point for a kaleidoscopic musical journey through time. It's a musical bridge back to the world of Mendelssohn's Violin Concerto, whose exploratory Romantic energy in turn propels us forwards to Mahler's Symphony No. 4. Infused with a love of nature and featuring a heart-rending slow movement, it concludes with a beguiling child's-eye view of heaven featuring Miah Persson as the soloist.

Spotlight on
Clara-Jumi Kang • Prom 24

'Mendelssohn never says, "No." It's always, "Yes, I do."' German-Korean violinist Clara-Jumi Kang is talking about her love for the directness and apparent effortlessness of the German composer's music. 'It has such a positive energy. I only enjoy his works more over time.' It's Mendelssohn's much-loved E minor Violin Concerto that Kang brings to the Proms on 3 August. Despite its countless performances since the 1845 premiere, Kang feels the piece never loses its freshness. 'My perspective on the music hasn't changed much over the years,' she admits, 'though my interpretation changes every time I play it. It's so special that you have so much freedom in Mendelssohn's music to put in your own personal touches.'

The performance marks Kang's Proms debut. It's an occasion she's been looking forward to enormously. 'I've admired the Proms since my early childhood. You can really feel the world coming together there. Especially in these difficult times, I'm so excited to experience music uniting people in this historic venue.' Kang's performance also marks a reunion between herself and conductor Ryan Bancroft, who conducted her performing the same concerto earlier this year. 'From my very first rehearsal with Ryan, I felt we both instinctively understood each other's musical language. It makes me so happy to discover new things with him during rehearsals, and also to have the trust and spontaneity onstage to try new aspects of the music too.'

Thursday 4 August

PROM 25
7.30pm–c9.55pm • Royal Albert Hall

⬤ £8.50–£42 *(plus booking fee*)*

JOHN STORGÅRDS

Kalevi Aho Eight Seasons
(Concerto for Theremin and
Chamber Orchestra)   *32'*
London premiere

INTERVAL

Kaija Saariaho Vista   *27'*

Shostakovich Symphony No. 15
in A major   *42'*

Carolina Eyck *theremin*

BBC Philharmonic
John Storgårds *conductor*

John Storgårds and the BBC Philharmonic
conjure up shifting colours and evocative
soundscapes in a programme rooted in
geography and identity. Finnish composer
Kalevi Aho's theremin concerto channels the
instrument's mysterious, almost shamanistic
quality in musical sketches of the eight
annual seasons observed by Lapland's Sámi
people, while Kaija Saariaho reflects broad
Californian views in the bold sonic gestures
of *Vista*. Surveying not a place but an entire
life, Shostakovich's final symphony offers a
dark, enigmatic conclusion to a career shaped
by conflict, political oppression and loss. *See
'Sounds Electric', pages 92–94.*

Friday 5 August

PROM 26
7.30pm–c9.45pm • Royal Albert Hall

⬤ £9.50–£52 *(plus booking fee*)*

KATIA AND MARIELLE LABÈQUE

Julian Anderson Symphony No. 2,
'Prague Panoramas'   *28'*
BBC co-commission: UK premiere

Martinů Concerto for Two Pianos   *23'*

INTERVAL

Rachmaninov Symphonic Dances *35'*

Katia and Marielle Labèque *pianos*

BBC Symphony Orchestra
Semyon Bychkov *conductor*

Whether it's the exhilarating propulsion of
Rachmaninov's *Symphonic Dances* or the lively
jazz and folk inflections of Martinů's Concerto
for Two Pianos, rhythm pulses through music
that emerged from the threat and brutality
of the Second World War. Czech composer
Martinů's wartime fears meet fellow exile
Rachmaninov's nostalgia for home in a heady
swirl of emotion. Semyon Bychkov conducts a
concert that opens with a major UK premiere by
Julian Anderson. Hailed by the *Financial Times*
as 'a 21st-century Debussy', Anderson here
finds inspiration in 1940s Prague, as captured in
Josef Sudek's haunting panoramic shots of the
city. *See 'Sound by Design', pages 64–67.*

Saturday 6 August

PROM 27
7.30pm–c9.35pm • Royal Albert Hall

⬤ £8.50–£42 *(plus booking fee*)*

ANDREW GOURLAY

Danny Elfman Wunderkammer   *20'*
London premiere

Gershwin, orch. Grofé Rhapsody
in Blue   *16'*

INTERVAL

Ravel Daphnis and Chloe   *50'*

Simone Dinnerstein *piano*

National Youth Orchestra of Great Britain
Andrew Gourlay *conductor*

Praised for its 'exuberant', 'exhilarating'
and 'thrilling' appearances at the Proms,
the National Youth Orchestra of Great Britain
returns for a concert that straddles stage
and screen, as well as the concert hall and
Hollywood. The sensuous radiance of Ravel's
ballet score *Daphnis and Chloe* – a 'vast musical
fresco' inspired by the ancient Greek story of
two foundlings who fall in love – meets the
electrifying, jazz-inspired energy of Gershwin's
Rhapsody in Blue. The concert opens with
the London premiere of *Wunderkammer*, a
kaleidoscopic new work from a film-music
legend: *Charlie and the Chocolate Factory* and
Edward Scissorhands composer Danny Elfman.

🖥 *Broadcast on BBC Four on Friday 19 August*

Sunday 7 August

PROM 28

3.00pm–*c*4.45pm • Royal Albert Hall

● £14–£62 *(plus booking fee')*

LEIF OVE ANDSNES

Mozart

| The Marriage of Figaro – overture | 5' |
| Piano Concerto No. 20 in D minor | 30' |

INTERVAL

| Piano Concerto No. 22 in E flat major | 34' |

Mahler Chamber Orchestra
Leif Ove Andsnes *piano/director*

Following on from their 'sensational' Beethoven Journey collaboration, the Mahler Chamber Orchestra and pianist Leif Ove Andsnes join forces again for an even more ambitious project. After four years of performances, recordings and festivals, their Mozart Momentum – a celebration of music from 1785 and 1786, two remarkable years in the composer's career – reaches its climax this season. In the first of three concerts *(see also Prom 29 and Proms at Battersea, 8 August)* the group brings together the stormy darkness of the composer's popular Piano Concerto No. 20 with the contrasting light and brilliance of the Concerto No. 22 – written alongside *The Marriage of Figaro*, whose bustling overture provides the evening's opener. *See 'Mozart at Close Quarters', pages 88–91; 'Full Steam Ahead', pages 100–103.*

⎕ *Broadcast on BBC Four tonight*

Sunday 7 August

PROM 29

7.30pm–*c*9.35pm • Royal Albert Hall

● £14–£62 *(plus booking fee')*

CHRISTIANE KARG

Mozart

Symphony No. 38 in D major, 'Prague'	22'
Three Songs: Die Zufriedenheit; Der Zauberer; Das Veilchen	8'
Concert Aria 'Ch'io mi scordi di te?'	10'

INTERVAL

| Masonic Funeral Music | 6' |
| Piano Concerto No. 24 in C minor | 31' |

Christiane Karg *soprano*

Mahler Chamber Orchestra
Leif Ove Andsnes *piano/director*

The second of three concerts from Leif Ove Andsnes and the Mahler Chamber Orchestra presents further highlights from their four-year Mozart Momentum project. Andsnes is both soloist and conductor, directing a sequence of songs and arias with soprano Christiane Karg, as well as the composer's sophisticated 'Prague' Symphony with its gamut of musical emotions – a triumphant follow-up to the success of *The Marriage of Figaro* – before moving to the keyboard for the chamber-music-like intimacy and conversational woodwind exchanges of the Piano Concerto No. 24. *See 'Mozart at Close Quarters', pages 88–91; 'Full Steam Ahead', pages 100–103.*

Spotlight on
Carolina Eyck • Prom 25

Lending its distinctive voice to countless sci-fi movie soundtracks, the theremin has an undeniable aura of the other-worldly. For German-born thereminist Carolina Eyck, however, it was simply the instrument she learnt as a child. 'My parents had been into electronic music and they introduced me to it,' she explains. 'I started playing when I was about 7.' Following studies with Russian theremin expert Lydia Kavina (a relative of the instrument's inventor, Leon Theremin), Eyck set about inventing her own playing technique – hardly a simple matter when a performer's hands never touch the instrument: 'I wanted to be more precise, so I used the width of my hand to measure the space more exactly: one hand-width equals an octave.'

It's a technique that Finnish composer Kalevi Aho exploits fully in *Eight Seasons*, the concerto he wrote for Eyck in 2011 and which she plays at her BBC Proms debut on 4 August. 'Kalevi really digs into the soul of the instrument,' says Eyck. 'But, when we were discussing the piece, I made the mistake of telling him I could sing and play at the same time, which he incorporated. It felt extremely complicated at first, but I'm more used to it now.' Still, it remains one of Eyck's favourite classical theremin pieces. 'I have a very melodic part with some quite theatrical, gestural playing. The piece ends in spring, with birdsong that I imitate on the theremin – it's almost as if I'm the shaman who's made that magic happen.'

Spotlight on
Ryan Bancroft
Proms 24 & 30

Becoming an orchestra's Principal Conductor in the middle of a pandemic is hardly straightforward, but that's what California-born Ryan Bancroft did with the BBC National Orchestra of Wales in 2020. 'In a funny way, we've been fortunate,' he explains. 'The groups I've been conducting have been so much smaller than usual that I've got to know the players much more quickly. I've made some serious bonds that I'd say are not just conductor to musician, but person to person.'

Nonetheless, he's excited to be back performing music for bigger forces, as he'll be doing with the BBC NOW in their two Proms, which feature Mahler's Fourth Symphony and Berlioz's *Symphonie fantastique* respectively. 'Berlioz calls for a massive number of musicians to tell his twisted story. It's safe to say we'll fill the stage. We've been discussing the bells he calls for in the final movement: if we use what Berlioz intended, the biggest one will weigh 1.5 tons!'

As a trumpet player himself, Bancroft is also excited to be conducting the premiere of Gavin Higgins's new Concerto Grosso for Brass Band and Orchestra. 'I played in symphonic wind bands in the US for many years, but only once have I conducted a brass band, in Carlisle. I know that brass band players are some of the most competitive people on the planet, so we'll need to make sure we're equally well prepared in the orchestra!'

Monday 8 August
PROMS AT BATTERSEA ☀
1.00pm–*c*2.00pm • Battersea Arts Centre

For ticket prices, see bbc.co.uk/promstickets

LEIF OVE ANDSNES

Mozart
Piano Trio in B flat major	22'
Piano Quartet in E flat major	27'

Leif Ove Andsnes *piano*

Members of the Mahler Chamber Orchestra
Matthew Truscott *violin*
Joel Hunter *viola*
Frank-Michael Guthmann *cello*

Leif Ove Andsnes and the Mahler Chamber Orchestra's Mozart Momentum project switches gear in this lunchtime recital, swapping concertos for chamber music. Andsnes is joined by members of the orchestra for Mozart's Piano Quartet in E flat major, whose affable, spacious character shares much with the Piano Concerto No. 22 *(see Prom 28)*. The Piano Trio in B flat major from the same year is a more extrovert affair – with a piano part almost concerto-like in its virtuosity. *See 'Mozart at Close Quarters', pages 88–91; 'Full Steam Ahead', pages 100–103.*

Every Prom live on BBC Radio 3 and available on BBC Sounds

Monday 8 August
PROM 30
7.00pm–*c*9.00pm • Royal Albert Hall

● **£9.50–£52** *(plus booking fee*)*

TREDEGAR BAND

Programme to include:

Gavin Higgins Concerto Grosso
for Brass Band and Orchestra   *c*25'
BBC commission: world premiere

INTERVAL

Berlioz Symphonie fantastique   49'

Tredegar Band
BBC National Orchestra of Wales
Ryan Bancroft *conductor*

A diabolical Witches' Sabbath, a ball, an unrequited passion and a march to the gallows make up the musical fever-dream of Berlioz's *Symphonie fantastique*. Inspired by the French composer's own romantic infatuation with a young Irish actress, the score is a cinematic fantasy full of tragedy and passion, a work teeming with orchestral drama and by turns gorgeous and grotesque. The BBC National Orchestra of Wales is joined by one of the country's leading brass bands, the Tredegar Band, for a new Concerto Grosso by Gavin Higgins that celebrates the brass band as part of Britain's cultural heritage.

Tuesday 9 August

PROM 31

7.00pm–c8.40pm • Royal Albert Hall

● £8.50–£42 *(plus booking fee')*

DANIELE RUSTIONI

Wagner Tannhäuser – Overture and Venusberg Music · 21'

R. Strauss Four Last Songs · 24'

Mahler Blumine · 8'

Schumann Symphony No. 4 in D minor · 28'

Louise Alder *soprano*

Ulster Orchestra
Daniele Rustioni *conductor*

There will be no interval

The Ulster Orchestra and Chief Conductor Daniele Rustioni take us from the physical to the metaphysical in a sumptuous celebration of German Romanticism. The Overture and Venusberg Music from Wagner's opera *Tannhäuser* plays out the drama's battle between the sensual and the spiritual in miniature, with restraint thrown to the wind in its heady Bacchanal *(See also Proms 55 and 72).* Darker themes come to the fore in Schumann's restless Symphony No. 4 and the yearning musical farewell of Strauss's *Four Last Songs*, performed here by Louise Alder, while Mahler's brief serenade *Blumine*, once part of his First Symphony, offers a moonlit moment of peace.

Tuesday 9 August

PROM 32 • LATE NIGHT ☾

10.15pm–c11.30pm • Royal Albert Hall

● £8.50–£26 *(plus booking fee')*

TREDEGAR BAND

R. Strauss, arr. Andrew Austin
Vienna Philharmonic Fanfare · 3'

Berlioz, arr. Geoffrey Brand
Overture 'Le corsaire' · 8'

Vaughan Williams, arr. Paul Hindmarsh Rhosymedre · 4'

Vaughan Williams, transcr. Phillip Littlemore Variations for brass band · 12'

Armengol, arr. Michael Pilley
Brassmen's Holiday · 2'

Philip Wilby Euphonium Concerto – Dance (Zeibekikos) · 3'

arr. **Andrew Austin**
Judy Garland Tribute · 6'

arr. **Malcolm Bennett**
MBC-7: Elmer Bernstein Tribute · 4'

Jim Root/Corey Taylor,
arr. Paul Saggers The Devil in I · 4'

Jimmy Webb, arr. Alan Catherall
MacArthur Park · 7'

Yu-Han Yang *euphonium*

Tredegar Band
Ian Porthouse *conductor*

There will be no interval

One of the world's great brass bands and stars of the BAFTA-winning film *Pride*, Wales's Tredegar Band takes in film music, show songs, classical and even heavy metal.

Spotlight on

Ian Porthouse • Prom 32

Few people are more immersed in Britain's proud brass band tradition than Ian Porthouse, conductor, cornet player, Director of Brass Band Studies at the Royal Birmingham Conservatoire and, since 2008, Music Director of South Wales's Tredegar Band, which gives two performances at this year's Proms. 'I'm actually from Cumbria, but my wife is from South Wales and plays in the band, as does my son, who's just starting his studies to be a professional musician.' There are more than 500 bands in the UK, he explains, 'and there can be a lot of intense rivalry. But that means we're all operating at an exceptionally high level.'

It's a level of virtuosity and musicianship that Porthouse is looking to demonstrate in the band's late-night Prom on 9 August. 'We're aiming to cover the history of brass band music in about an hour!' he laughs. The previous evening, the band has a single focus, joining the BBC National Orchestra of Wales to premiere a new piece by Gavin Higgins. 'I've actually known Gavin since he played in the National Youth Brass Band of Great Britain, where I was a cornet tutor. He's always had a deep passion for brass band music: he wrote a competition piece for Tredegar in 2011, and *Dark Arteries* for us and Rambert in 2015. This must be the first major piece written for brass band and orchestra. I've done a lot of orchestral playing, but to sit in the middle of the band, surrounded by a huge symphony orchestra – it's going to feel amazing.'

Spotlight on
Kian Soltani • Prom 34

'You could almost imagine the piece representing life itself.' Austrian-Iranian cellist Kian Soltani is considering Elgar's Cello Concerto, which he performs at the Proms on 11 August. It's a piece he knows well: 'For me, it has a lot to do with fate. It starts with a vision – the iconic opening theme that's introduced by the solo cello, and which reappears at the very end. From there it starts telling a story, one of passion, reflection and dialogue. The idea of the concerto is born in the first movement. The second movement feels like an attempt to escape reality – it has a child-like naivety. The third brings us back to reality: it's a story of love and loss, sung amid tears.' For Soltani, the finale represents confrontation. 'Here, more than in any other movement, the cellist has a dialogue with the orchestra, sometimes disagreeing, sometimes joining in. It culminates in a dramatic climax that brings back a distant memory of the third movement, then the fateful first theme.'

What does this underlying narrative mean for Soltani's playing? 'The challenge lies in telling a story from the first note to the last, keeping that overarching line. Through the ups and downs, I always need to keep the big picture in mind.' And, if the concerto charts the course of a life, what does that mean for the work's famously profound and powerful ending? 'It's as if one cannot escape one's own fate, no matter how one tries. The final bars are either victory or defeat – however you want to see it.'

Wednesday 10 August

PROM 33
7.30pm–c9.50pm • Royal Albert Hall

🔘 £9.50–£52 *(plus booking fee*)*

RODERICK WILLIAMS

R. Strauss Death and Transfiguration   23'
Matthew Kaner Pearl   c25'
BBC commission: world premiere

INTERVAL

Holst The Planets   51'

Roderick Williams *baritone*

BBC Symphony Chorus
BBC Symphony Orchestra
Ryan Wigglesworth *conductor*

From broad visions of the universe to the intimacy of human relationships, the wonder of creation to the fragile moment of death, Ryan Wigglesworth and the BBC Symphony Orchestra and Chorus take us through it all. Human loss is at the heart both of Strauss's tender, rapturous tone-poem *Death and Transfiguration* – an orchestral portrait of 'the dying hours of a man' – and of Matthew Kaner's *Pearl*, a lament whose medieval text sees a grieving father glimpsing his daughter in the afterlife. Holst's *The Planets* leaves Earth far behind in its vivid, myth-inspired journey through our solar system in all its mysterious beauty.

Thursday 11 August

PROM 34
7.30pm–c9.45pm • Royal Albert Hall

🔘 £9.50–£52 *(plus booking fee*)*

EVA OLLIKAINEN

Anna Thorvaldsdottir
ARCHORA   c20'
BBC co-commission: world premiere

Elgar Cello Concerto in E minor   27'

INTERVAL

Sibelius Symphony No. 2 in D major   43'

Kian Soltani *cello*

BBC Philharmonic
Eva Ollikainen *conductor*

Primal urges – to live, love and be free – animate this concert from Eva Ollikainen and the BBC Philharmonic. Elgar's Cello Concerto combines a deep sense of mourning – possibly at the catastrophe of the First World War – with the most heartfelt, eloquent lyricism, while echoes of both Don Juan and Dante's *Divine Comedy* are woven through Sibelius's Second Symphony, a work torn between pastoral calm and restless disquiet, and later adopted as a symbol of Finnish national resistance and liberation. Award-winning Icelandic composer Anna Thorvaldsdottir's music has a tectonic quality, cracking and flickering with elemental force. Primordial energy itself is the inspiration for her *ARCHORA*, which receives its world premiere.

🖥 *Broadcast on BBC Four on Sunday 14 August*

Friday 12 August

PROM 35
7.30pm–c9.45pm • Royal Albert Hall

● £14–£62 (plus booking fee')

KLAUS MÄKELÄ

Sibelius Tapiola   19'
Liszt Piano Concerto No. 1
in E flat major   19'

INTERVAL

R. Strauss Ein Heldenleben   45'

Yuja Wang piano

Oslo Philharmonic
Klaus Mäkelä conductor

From the battle between soloist and orchestra
that opens Liszt's Piano Concerto No. 1 to
the autobiographical strivings and yearnings
of Strauss's *Ein Heldenleben* ('A Hero's Life'),
Romantic urgency courses through this
Prom from the Oslo Philharmonic and Chief
Conductor Klaus Mäkelä. Piano sensation Yuja
Wang is the soloist in Liszt's mould-breaking
concerto – pianistic brilliance meeting formal
innovation with explosive results – while the
orchestra takes centre stage in two great
tone-poems, setting the cool, mythic forests
of Sibelius's *Tapiola*, with their 'magic secrets'
and 'wood sprites', against the human heat of
life and love in *Ein Heldenleben*. See 'Full Steam
Ahead', pages 100–103.

🖥 *Broadcast on BBC Four tonight*

Saturday 13 August

PROM 36
7.30pm–c9.50pm • Royal Albert Hall

● £14–£62 (plus booking fee')

MARIN ALSOP

Bartók The Miraculous Mandarin –
suite   19'
Prokofiev Piano Concerto No. 3
in C major   27'

INTERVAL

Hannah Eisendle Heliosis   8'
UK premiere

Dvořák Symphony No. 7
in D minor   35'

Benjamin Grosvenor piano

Vienna Radio Symphony Orchestra
Marin Alsop conductor

Marin Alsop and the Vienna Radio Symphony
Orchestra are joined by Proms regular and
former BBC Radio 3 New Generation Artist
Benjamin Grosvenor for Prokofiev's ferociously
demanding Piano Concerto No. 3. 'My new
symphony,' wrote Dvořák of his Seventh,
'must … make a stir in the world.' The result
does just that, emerging from a brooding
opening into rhapsodic warmth, animated by
folk dances and a seemingly endless stream of
melodies. This contrasts with the deliciously
grotesque episodes of Bartók's *The Miraculous
Mandarin* suite; and tonight's orchestra and
conductor also bring a new work by Viennese
composer Hannah Eisendle, having given its
premiere in March. *See 'Rolling with the Punches',
pages 20–24; 'Full Steam Ahead', pages 100–103.*

🖥 *Broadcast on BBC Four on Sunday 21 August*

Spotlight on
Yuja Wang • Prom 35

'I love that the Prommers shout out "Heave
ho!" when the stage team raise the piano
lid – it's the only place in the world for that!'
Pianist Yuja Wang is no stranger to the
Proms, and gets an undeniable thrill from
performing at the festival: 'You feel like a
rock star.' It's music by another rock star –
or the 19th century's equivalent, perhaps –
that Wang performs on 12 August: the First
Piano Concerto by Franz Liszt. 'I remember
playing it when I was 17,' she says. 'It was
my debut with the New York Philharmonic,
conducted by Lorin Maazel in Tokyo. It's
interesting to pick up works again: the
notes are still in the muscle memory, but
other layers and characters in the music are
revealed.' The concerto's cascades of notes
are just one of its challenges. 'Liszt's swift
and sudden mood changes are often very
flirty and charming, and one challenge is
maintaining tension so that the audience
can follow the form of the piece. I have to
think of myself as an actor, and to be in
character to pull off the best performance.'

Wang was due to collaborate with the Oslo
Philharmonic and conductor Klaus Mäkelä,
her Proms co-performers, in August last
year, but Covid restrictions made it
impossible. 'The pandemic was a big event
for me – and for everyone. I didn't touch
a piano for a year. I tried lots of different
things, including cooking, which it turns
out I have no talent for! A huge part of my
art is playing for an audience – I've really
missed it. And wearing heels!'

Sunday 14 August

PROM 37 ☀

11.00am–c12.40pm • Royal Albert Hall

● £8.50–£42 *(plus booking fee')*

NICHOLAS DANIEL

Haydn Symphony No. 6 in D major, 'Le matin'　20'

Vaughan Williams
Oboe Concerto　19'

Kaija Saariaho Vers toi qui es si loin　7'
London premiere

Beethoven Symphony No. 4
in B flat major　34'

There will be no interval

Nicholas Daniel *oboe*
Maria Włoszczowska *violin*

Royal Northern Sinfonia
Dinis Sousa *conductor*

Celebrations of Vaughan Williams's 150th anniversary continue with the Royal Northern Sinfonia and Principal Conductor Dinis Sousa. They are joined by soloist Nicholas Daniel for the Oboe Concerto – a work that opens in elegiac, pastoral sweetness but also explores the instrument's piquant wit and athleticism. The music's echoes of medieval chant are shared by Kaija Saariaho's *Vers toi qui es si loin* – a mesmerising, other-worldly adaptation of music from the composer's troubadour opera *L'amour de loin*, with the original soprano line reassigned to a solo violin, played in her Proms debut by Polish violinist Maria Włoszczowska. This leads into Beethoven's Fourth Symphony, a joyful, energetic work often overshadowed by its two heavyweight symphonic neighbours.
See 'The Shape of British Music', pages 44–49.

Sunday 14 August

PROM 38

7.30pm–c9.45pm • Royal Albert Hall

● £9.50–£52 *(plus booking fee')*

JENNIFER KOH

Tchaikovsky Swan Lake – suite　23'
Missy Mazzoli Violin Concerto, 'Procession'　20'
BBC co-commission: European premiere

INTERVAL

Prokofiev
Romeo and Juliet – excerpts　45'

Jennifer Koh *violin*

Philharmonia Orchestra
Santtu-Matias Rouvali *conductor*

The Philharmonia Orchestra makes its first Proms appearance under Principal Conductor Santtu-Matias Rouvali with highlights from two classic Russian ballets that combine star-crossed lovers and intervening forces in their different ways. Death – tragic, macabre, but also blackly comic – hangs over Missy Mazzoli's Violin Concerto, 'Procession': Jennifer Koh is the soloist in the European premiere of a piece that looks back to the funeral rituals of medieval Europe during the Black Death.
See 'Mood Music', pages 72–77.

Every Prom live on BBC Radio 3 and available on BBC Sounds

Monday 15 August

📍 PROMS AT **CARDIFF** ☀

1.00pm–c2.00pm • Royal Welsh College of Music & Drama, Dora Stoutzker Hall

For ticket prices, see bbc.co.uk/promstickets

CARION WIND QUINTET

Ligeti Bagatelles　12'
Nielsen Wind Quintet　27'
Stravinsky, arr. David M. A. P. Palmquist
Suite No. 2　6'

Carion Wind Quintet

The prize-winning Danish-Latvian Carion Wind Quintet has won acclaim for its 'dramatised' chamber music performances. Performing every concert from memory and presenting each work as a fully choreographed fusion of sound and movement, the group aims to add a new dimension to the traditional concert format. Here the ensemble brings its signature style to Ligeti's vibrantly pithy *Bagatelles*, Nielsen's characterful Wind Quintet (its individual parts all shaped for friends of the composer) and Stravinsky's similarly playful, satirical Suite No. 2 for small orchestra, arranged for wind quintet.

20 Proms on BBC TV and available on BBC iPlayer

Monday 15 August

PROM 39
7.30pm–c9.40pm • Royal Albert Hall

⬤ £8.50–£42 (plus booking fee')

CONSTANTIN HARTWIG

Mark-Anthony Turnage
Time Flies 24'
BBC co-commission: UK premiere

Vaughan Williams
Tuba Concerto 13'

INTERVAL

Elgar Symphony No. 1
in A flat major 50'

Constantin Hartwig *tuba*

BBC Symphony Orchestra
Sakari Oramo *conductor*

A concert of English music continues this
season's strand of concertos for instruments
often shunned from the limelight. International
prize-winner Constantin Hartwig is the soloist
in Vaughan Williams's Tuba Concerto – the
first of its kind for the instrument, a work with
a twinkle in its eye that catches the tuba's
bluff, Falstaffian bluster. Many years in the
making, Elgar's First Symphony is an optimistic
work, bursting with melody and emotion,
expressing 'a massive hope in the future'. It's
a mood shared with Mark-Anthony Turnage's
celebratory *Time Flies*, inspired by the feats of
the Olympics. See 'The Shape of British Music',
pages 44–49.

Tuesday 16 August

PROM 40
7.30pm–c9.40pm • Royal Albert Hall

⬤ £9.50–£52 (plus booking fee')

VASILY PETRENKO

Copland Appalachian Spring –
suite 24'

Walker Trombone Concerto 17'

INTERVAL

Prokofiev Symphony No. 5
in B flat major 46'

Peter Moore *trombone*

Royal Philharmonic Orchestra
Vasily Petrenko *conductor*

Following his award-winning Prokofiev
symphony cycle with the Oslo Philharmonic,
conductor Vasily Petrenko and the Royal
Philharmonic Orchestra bring the composer's
wartime Symphony No. 5 to the Proms. The
music's hope for the 'free and happy' human
soul is tempered by twitching martial rhythms
and louring brass threats. An all-American
first half features the delicate, folk-infused
nationalism of Copland's *Appalachian Spring*
suite, followed by the bluesy colours and
jazz-inspired rhythms of centenary composer
George Walker's 1957 Trombone Concerto.
*See 'Rolling with the Punches', pages 20–24;
'A World of Music', pages 36–38.*

Spotlight on
Peter Moore • Prom 40

'I always think to myself that a composer
like Rachmaninov could have written a
great trombone concerto.' Peter Moore
is mulling over his instrument's concerto
repertoire and the relative scarcity of
major works for trombone and orchestra.
'We almost had one by Mendelssohn.
But the story goes that at the last minute
he passed it over to the leader of his
orchestra, Ferdinand David, and it became
his *Concertino*.' That's why, Moore says,
he's always been interested in new pieces
for trombone. 'But of course we also have
to look back to the past and rediscover
some of the lesser-known works.'

One of those is the piece Moore performs
on 16 August: the 1957 Trombone Concerto
by George Walker, the Black American
composer whose centenary is celebrated
across the Proms this year. 'It's extremely
well written for the instrument: he clearly
had a great understanding of what projects.
It's going to be a dream to perform in the
Royal Albert Hall.' Although it's Moore's
debut as a Proms soloist, it's far from his
first Prom. He's performed among the
ranks of several orchestras, including the
London Symphony, where he was appointed
Co-Principal Trombone aged 18, and is now
Principal. 'I had quite an unusual beginning,
starting as a soloist before becoming an
orchestral player too. Playing in a great
orchestra over the past few years has
transformed me as a musician, and it all
feeds into the way I play as a soloist as well.'

Spotlight on

Behzod Abduraimov
Prom 41

'It was a blast!' Uzbek pianist Behzod Abduraimov is remembering the last time he performed with the BBC Scottish Symphony Orchestra and conductor Thomas Dausgaard, his collaborators at the Proms this year. In 2018 they played Rachmaninov's Third Piano Concerto. 'I remember it well,' he continues. 'Thomas was very attentive to the composer's intentions while also accommodating my own interpretation. It was a pure joy.'

It's an entirely different piece that they perform on 17 August. To some, Beethoven's First Piano Concerto is a cap-doffing to Haydn and Mozart. For others, the young composer is staking out his own distinctive musical territory. 'For me, it's both,' says Abduraimov. 'It was written after the Second Piano Concerto, so you can already hear Beethoven's typical depth of harmony, in very much his own style, as well as influences from Mozart's operas and Haydn's humour.'

Though it doesn't demand Rachmaninov's fistfuls of notes, Beethoven's First Concerto has challenges of its own. 'You have to be flexible enough to find an ideal balance between the orchestra and the soloist, especially in the poetic second movement. The interpretation has to be almost like chamber music. But the festive character and vivid colours of the first movement, the soulful dialogues between piano and woodwind in the second and the humorous final rondo make the piece very inspiring.'

Wednesday 17 August

PROM 41
7.30pm–c9.40pm • Royal Albert Hall

⬤ £9.50–£52 *(plus booking fee*)*

ELIZABETH WATTS

Ravel La valse   12'
Beethoven Piano Concerto No. 1 in C major   36'
INTERVAL
Nielsen Symphony No. 3, 'Sinfonia espansiva'   39'

Behzod Abduraimov *piano*
Elizabeth Watts *soprano*
Benjamin Appl *baritone*

BBC Scottish Symphony Orchestra
Thomas Dausgaard *conductor*

Waltzes whirl through this programme, as the BBC Scottish Symphony Orchestra and its Chief Conductor Thomas Dausgaard present the first of two consecutive Proms pairing one of Carl Nielsen's groundbreaking symphonies with one of Beethoven's eloquent piano concertos. A 'cosmic waltz' propels us onto a powerful, elemental trajectory in Nielsen's Third Symphony, before nature takes a simpler, more bucolic form in the later movements. Solos from British soprano Elizabeth Watts and German-British baritone Benjamin Appl provide the climax to the sumptuous second movement. Ravel's dizzying *La valse* captures the heightened pleasures and tragic collapse of Vienna. Behzod Abduraimov – described by *The Independent* as 'the most perfectly accomplished pianist of his generation' – is the soloist in Beethoven's First Piano Concerto.

Thursday 18 August

PROM 42
7.30pm–c9.50pm • Royal Albert Hall

⬤ £9.50–£52 *(plus booking fee*)*

FRANCESCO PIEMONTESI

Sibelius Symphony No. 7 in C major   22'
Beethoven Piano Concerto No. 4 in G major   35'
INTERVAL
Nielsen Symphony No. 4, 'The Inextinguishable'   36'

Francesco Piemontesi *piano*

BBC Scottish Symphony Orchestra
Thomas Dausgaard *conductor*

'Music is like life and, like life, inextinguishable,' wrote Carl Nielsen. It's this broad philosophy that underpins his ambitious Symphony No. 4 – a work that hurls us from conflict to magnificent resolution. In the second of their two concerts together, Thomas Dausgaard and the BBC Scottish Symphony Orchestra continue to explore Denmark's great symphonist, here set alongside his Finnish contemporary Sibelius, whose remarkable Symphony No. 7 unfolds in a single movement – a unified, and ultimately triumphant, musical vision. Former BBC Radio 3 New Generation Artist Francesco Piemontesi is the soloist in Beethoven's Piano Concerto No. 4 – acting as Orpheus taming the orchestral Furies in the evocative central movement.

Friday 19 August

PROM 43

7.00pm–c10.05pm • Royal Albert Hall

⬤ £9.50–£52 *(plus booking fee*)*

JOÉLLE HARVEY

Handel Solomon

145'

Cast to include:

Iestyn Davies *Solomon*
Joélle Harvey *Solomon's Queen/First Harlot*
Benjamin Hulett *Zadok*
Ashley Riches *A Levite*

BBC Singers
The English Concert
Sofi Jeannin *conductor*

There will be one interval

The Proms's ongoing sequence of Handel oratorios continues with *Solomon*. Sofi Jeannin conducts early music specialists The English Concert in this mature masterpiece that combines operatic drama with spiritual solemnity in its retelling of the story of the wise King Solomon. The exhilarating 'Arrival of the Queen of Sheba' is just one highlight in a work whose intricate choral writing and richly varied orchestration combine in a score of breadth and beauty. American soprano Joélle Harvey and British counter-tenor Iestyn Davies lead an all-star cast.

Every Prom live on BBC Radio 3 and available on BBC Sounds

Saturday 20 August

PROM 44

7.30pm–c9.30pm • Royal Albert Hall

⬤ £8.50–£42 *(plus booking fee*)*

NARDUS WILLIAMS

Debussy Nocturnes

24'

INTERVAL

Smyth Mass in D major

60'

Nardus Williams *soprano*
Bethan Langford *mezzo-soprano*
Robert Murray *tenor*
Božidar Smiljanić *bass-baritone*

BBC Symphony Chorus
BBC Symphony Orchestra
Sakari Oramo *conductor*

Sacred and secular drift and blur into one another in the twilight visions of Debussy's three orchestral *Nocturnes*. Sirens coax and seduce sailors with their mysterious song, while back on land a festive parade is all brilliant flashes of light and teeming, fleet-footed movement. But the opening cloudscape looks heavenwards in its plainchant-inspired lines – a prelude to Ethel Smyth's Mass in D major, whose bold, robust expression of faith owes as much to Beethoven as to Elgar, and couldn't be further from Debussy's hazy sonic watercolours. Sakari Oramo conducts the BBC Symphony Chorus and Orchestra and an exciting team of young soloists including soprano Nardus Williams and bass-baritone Božidar Smiljanić. *See 'The Shape of British Music', pages 44–49.*

Spotlight on

Sofi Jeannin • Prom 43

From an era-straddling collaboration with turntablist Shiva Feshareki last year to a performance of Handel's lavish oratorio *Solomon* this year: you could never accuse the BBC Singers of being short-sighted in their repertoire or their ambitions. 'That's why they're such an exciting group,' says the Singers' Chief Conductor Sofi Jeannin. 'We have to be the ambassadors for singing, and for the pure joy of singing in a choir.'

This year Jeannin conducts the Singers alongside the period players of The English Concert. 'This is actually my first time conducting *Solomon*,' she explains. 'I've known it well since I was a student, though my understanding of it has developed a lot since then. It's Handel at his best, and it's remarkable that it took him just six weeks to compose. For me, it represents Handel's brilliance as a dramatist.'

To what extent does Jeannin feel Handel moulded his expertise in opera into this new form? 'Let's not forget that by the time he wrote *Solomon* he'd left Italian opera behind him. Biblical stories were not permitted in London's opera houses, and so Handel developed the English oratorio, based on similar formats from the continent. But of course this is first and foremost a dramatic work, and it's easy to hear the incredible dramatic tension Handel creates. We'll be wanting to make sure the story jumps off the page, whether listeners are in the Hall with us or listening on the radio around the world.'

Sunday 21 August

PROM 45 ☀
11.30am–c1.00pm • Royal Albert Hall

● £8.50–£42 (plus booking fee')

AMJAD ALI KHAN

Amjad Ali Khan sarod
Amaan Ali Bangash sarod/vocals
Ayaan Ali Bangash sarod

There will be no interval

Combining the rhythmic energy of the guitar with the expressive, singing quality of the human voice, the sarod is a defining sound of Indian classical music. One of the undisputed masters of the instrument, whose career spans more than six decades, Amjad Ali Khan is joined here by his sons Amaan Ali Bangash and Ayaan Ali Bangash, as well as leading exponents of the tabla and mridangam for a celebration of this versatile and expressive instrument. *See 'Master and Student', pages 68–70.*

Every Prom live on BBC Radio 3 and available on BBC Sounds

Sunday 21 August

PROM 46
7.30pm–c9.40pm • Royal Albert Hall

● £14–£62 (plus booking fee')

AUGUSTIN HADELICH

Mendelssohn Overture 'The Hebrides' ('Fingal's Cave')   10'
Dvořák Violin Concerto in A minor   32'

INTERVAL

Brahms Symphony No. 3 in F major   37'

Augustin Hadelich violin

WDR Symphony Orchestra Cologne
Cristian Măcelaru conductor

This season's celebration of great international radio orchestras continues with Cologne's WDR Symphony Orchestra and its Chief Conductor Cristian Măcelaru. 'From start to finish one is wrapped about with the mysterious charm of the woods and forests. I could not tell you which movement I loved most,' wrote Clara Schumann of Brahms's Symphony No. 3 – a work whose concealed musical motto, 'Free but happy', sets the tone for its striving energy and intimacy. Grammy-winning violinist Augustin Hadelich is the soloist in Dvořák's Violin Concerto, whose forthright opening gives way to a luscious slow movement and, finally, a whirling dance of a rondo. Opening the Prom is Mendelssohn's ever-popular concert overture *The Hebrides*, inspired by Scotland's rugged coastline. *See 'Full Steam Ahead', pages 100–103.*

Monday 22 August

📍 PROMS AT **LIVERPOOL** ☀
1.00pm–c2.00pm • St George's Hall

For ticket prices, see bbc.co.uk/promstickets

DUDOK QUARTET AMSTERDAM

Carwithen String Quartet No. 2   20'
Brahms String Quartet in A minor, Op. 51 No. 2   34'

Dudok Quartet Amsterdam

Praised for its 'virtuosity, finesse and coursing energy', the prize-winning Dudok Quartet Amsterdam makes its Proms debut, pairing music by Brahms with the Second String Quartet by British composer Doreen Carwithen. One hundred years on from her birth, Carwithen – a successful film-music composer, whose works were admired by Vaughan Williams – is finally claiming her rightful place in the concert hall. Her award-winning quartet has echoes of Bartók in its knotty lyricism and elegiac intensity. Tensions, doubts and uncertainties animate Brahms's mature Second String Quartet, with turbulence and passion never far below the surface. *See 'The Shape of British Music', pages 44–49.*

Monday 22 August

PROM 47
7.30pm–c9.30pm • Royal Albert Hall

● **£14–£62** *(plus booking fee')*

SHELÉA

Aretha Franklin: Queen of Soul

Sheléa

Jules Buckley Orchestra
Jules Buckley *conductor*

There will be one interval

In her 80th-anniversary year – and 50 years since the release of her album *Young, Gifted and Black* – the Proms pays tribute to the 'Queen of Soul', Aretha Franklin. A singer, songwriter, pianist and one of the best-selling recording artists of all time, whose song 'Respect' became an anthem of the American Civil Rights Movement, Franklin is remembered in a unique Prom featuring a collection of her greatest hits with a dynamic orchestral backing. Jules Buckley conducts his newly formed ensemble in its Proms debut, joined by American singer-songwriter and Quincy Jones protégée Sheléa. *See 'Aretha, Queen of Soul', pages 14–16.*

📺 *Broadcast on BBC Four on Friday 26 August*

20 Proms on BBC TV and available on BBC iPlayer

Tuesday 23 August

PROM 48
7.30pm–c9.35pm • Royal Albert Hall

● **£9.50–£52** *(plus booking fee')*

SIOBHAN STAGG

Webern
Passacaglia, Op. 1   11'
Six Pieces for Orchestra, Op. 6
(revised version, 1928)   13'

Debussy, arr. Brett Dean
Ariettes oubliées   16'

INTERVAL

Brahms Symphony No. 2
in D major   43'

Siobhan Stagg *soprano*

Australian World Orchestra
Zubin Mehta *conductor*

Celebrated conductor Zubin Mehta returns to the Proms for the first time in over a decade. He marks 2022's UK/Australia Season cultural initiative with the Australian World Orchestra – a classical supergroup whose members are drawn from some 50 of the world's greatest international orchestras. Brahms's lyrical Second Symphony – clouds gathering just beneath its sunny surface – is prefaced by a sequence of early works by two starkly contrasting composers. The lushness of Webern's Op. 1 *Passacaglia* gives way to the spare textures and telling gestures of the *Six Pieces for Orchestra*, while the Verlaine song-cycle *Ariettes oubliées* sees Debussy forging the expressive, speech-song word-setting that would redefine opera in *Pelléas and Mélisande*. *See 'Rolling with the Punches', pages 20–24; 'Full Steam Ahead', pages 100–103.*

Spotlight on
Amjad Ali Khan • Prom 45

'Learning Indian classical music is a long journey. It's like an elephant walking – you must undertake the journey with grace and dignity.' For Indian sarod maestro Amjad Ali Khan, it's been a lifelong pursuit: he learnt from his father Hafiz Ali Khan, and in turn taught his sons Amaan Ali Bangash and Ayaan Ali Bangash. 'We are all soloists, and often they perform on their own,' he continues, 'but on special occasions the three of us get together to perform.' One such occasion is at the Proms on 21 August – his second appearance at the festival. 'My Proms debut was in 1994. I have a special feeling for England – and obviously the BBC has had a long association with India, too.'

Khan is one of the world's most respected Indian classical musicians as well as a great innovator, both within his tradition and in Western crossover styles. 'Unfortunately the world blindly follows convention. But there's a difference between convention and tradition: tradition allows innovation. I respect tradition, but not convention.' Can Khan see his own musical personality in the way his sons play? 'The music of certain families in India sounds identical. But our approach is different. Amaan and Ayaan have their own ways of playing. I've always encouraged them to listen to any kind of music they wanted to.' And does he enjoy performing alongside them now? 'Very much – and, of course, they like to surprise me when we play together!'

Wednesday 24 August

PROM 49

7.00pm–c8.35pm • Royal Albert Hall

● £18–£72 *(plus booking fee')*

LOUISE ALDER

Sir Harrison Birtwistle Donum Simoni MMXVIII 4'

Mahler Symphony No. 2 in C minor, 'Resurrection' 80'

Louise Alder *soprano*
Dame Sarah Connolly *mezzo-soprano*

CBSO Chorus
London Symphony Chorus
London Symphony Orchestra
Sir Simon Rattle *conductor*

There will be no interval

With its vast performing forces and huge soundscapes, Mahler's Second Symphony deals with no less a subject than the meaning of life. Wrestling with doubts and questions of human purpose, happiness and death, it offers extraordinary consolation in its final two movements, closing with a rapturous affirmation of faith: 'I shall soar upwards, I shall die in order to live.' Opening the concert is Sir Harrison Birtwistle's rousing *Donum Simoni MMXVIII* for wind, brass and percussion – a musical gift composed in 2018 especially for Sir Simon Rattle and the London Symphony Orchestra.

▢ *Broadcast on BBC Four on Sunday 28 August*

Wednesday 24 August

PROM 50 • LATE NIGHT ☾

10.15pm–c11.30pm • Royal Albert Hall

● £8.50–£26 *(plus booking fee')*

THE SIXTEEN

Plainsong 'Salve Regina' 3'

Tavener A Hymn to the Mother of God 3'

Tallis Spem in alium 10'

Sir James MacMillan Miserere 12'

Tye Missa 'Euge bone' – Agnus Dei 7'

Górecki Totus tuus 9'

Sheppard Missa 'Cantate' – Agnus Dei 5'

Sir James MacMillan Vidi aquam 10'

Byrd Diliges Dominum 3'

The Sixteen
Harry Christophers *conductor*

There will be no interval

Leading professional chamber choir The Sixteen returns to the Proms with Artistic Director Harry Christophers for a late-night musical meditation bridging the Renaissance and the present day. Thomas Tallis's magnificent 40-part motet *Spem in alium* and Sir James MacMillan's contemporary companion piece for the same forces, *Vidi aquam*, are the twin pillars of a concert that also includes music by Tallis's Tudor contemporaries Byrd, Sheppard and Tye, as well as John Tavener's radiant *A Hymn to the Mother of God* and Górecki's hypnotic choral prayer *Totus tuus*.

Thursday 25 August

PROM 51

7.30pm–c9.40pm • Royal Albert Hall

● £8.50–£42 *(plus booking fee')*

FABIEN GABEL

Lalo Le roi d'Ys – overture 11'

Brahms Violin Concerto in D major 38'

INTERVAL

Franck Symphony in D minor 37'

Daniel Lozakovich *violin*

BBC Symphony Orchestra
Fabien Gabel *conductor*

Franz Liszt declared César Franck's organ works to be worthy of 'a place beside the masterpieces of Bach', and it's the organ's thick sonorities and glowing weight that seem to lie behind the composer's mature Symphony in D minor – a work of contrasts, which opens in almost Wagnerian grandeur and closes with a radiant finale. Music by Franck's French contemporary Édouard Lalo opens the concert – the stirring, filmic overture to his medieval Breton opera *Le roi d'Ys*. At just 21, the Swedish violinist Daniel Lozakovich is a major new talent, and makes his Proms debut as soloist in one of the great Romantic violin concertos. Fabien Gabel conducts the BBC Symphony Orchestra.

Friday 26 August

PROM 52
7.30pm–c9.25pm • Royal Albert Hall

● **£14–£62** (plus booking fee*)

PEKKA KUUSISTO

Vaughan Williams The Lark
Ascending   13'
Debussy La mer   23'

INTERVAL

Thomas Adès Märchentänze   13'
UK premiere
Sibelius Symphony No. 5
in E flat major   30'

Pekka Kuusisto violin

Finnish Radio Symphony Orchestra
Nicholas Collon conductor

A lone bird soars and dives in Vaughan
Williams's *The Lark Ascending*; a whole chorus
of skylarks come together in joyful clamour
in Thomas Adès's *Märchentänze* ('Fairy-Tale
Dances'); and swans fly, majestic in Sibelius's
Symphony No. 5. Nature – beautiful, powerful,
elemental – is the guiding thread through this
concert from the Finnish Radio Symphony
Orchestra and Nicholas Collon, taking us from
the English countryside to the glitter and
churn of waves in Debussy's *La mer* and finally
to Finland's forests and lakes. Finnish violin
maverick Pekka Kuusisto is the soloist. *See 'The
Shape of British Music', pages 44–49; 'Full Steam
Ahead', pages 100–103; 'Behold … The Sea!',
pages 104–107.*

Saturday 27 August

PROMS 53 & 54
2.00pm–c4.00pm & 7.30pm–c9.30pm
Royal Albert Hall   ☀

● **£14–£62** (plus booking fee*)

Earth Prom

BBC Scottish Symphony Orchestra
Ben Palmer conductor

AD *2.00pm performance audio-described by
Timna Fibert*
BSL *2.00pm performance British Sign Language-
interpreted by Angie Newman*

Across seas and mountains, rivers, glaciers
and deserts … in the centenary year of the
BBC the Proms brings a musical celebration
of the world-famous BBC Studios Natural
History Unit through the ages – from David
Attenborough's early adventures to the
present. This spectacular audio-visual journey
features soaring scores by composers including
Hans Zimmer and George Fenton, and music
from around the globe, as well as the sounds of
nature, breathtaking imagery and spoken word.

📻 *Broadcast live on BBC Radio 3 (Prom 54)*

📺 *Broadcast on BBC Two on Monday 29 August
(Prom 54)*

**20 Proms on
BBC TV and
available on
BBC iPlayer**

Spotlight on
Daniel Lozakovich • Prom 51

'Playing this concerto felt like being on top
of a mountain.' Quite literally for Swedish
violinist Daniel Lozakovich, who's looking
back on his performance of Brahms's Violin
Concerto at the Verbier Festival high in the
Swiss Alps last autumn. But Lozakovich
is referring more to the work's spiritual
dimension. 'It's as if the music comes
from a higher state. It's transcendental,
with deep emotions and a lot of love. You
have to live the piece rather than just
play it – dedicate yourself to the music,
and feel like you're in the same emotional
state as Brahms when he wrote it.'

Lozakovich brings the piece to the Proms
on 25 August, and his recent performances
represent reaching a summit in other ways,
too. 'My favourite recording when I was
very young was Brahms's Violin Concerto
performed by David Oistrakh. It was one
of the first things to inspire me to take up
the violin. Then I'd just started learning
the concerto at the start of the pandemic –
which ironically gave me a lot of time to
study it. So performing a concerto I'd had
in my brain since I was a kid, and finally
being back onstage after such a long time,
has been incredible – and good for my soul.'

From the top of a mountain to an
iconic concert venue in central London:
Lozakovich is delighted to be making
his Proms debut. 'I've known about
these legendary concerts since I first
started listening to classical music. So
to perform here is a dream come true.'

Spotlight on
Nathan Laube • Prom 55

When Chicago-born organist Nathan Laube steps up to the console of the Royal Albert Hall's mighty Willis organ on 28 August, he'll be making his debut at the Proms. But not, he reveals, in the Hall itself. 'In 2010 a friend arranged for a small group of us to have a full night alone in the Hall to explore the instrument. These "all-nighters" are actually a fairly typical ritual. It was an extraordinary experience exploring the nearly 150 stops, taking turns to play and listen from various points around the Hall, getting a sense of how that beast behaves.'

And it will have served him well, no doubt, as preparation for his Proms recital. As well as works by Franck and Alkan, the former conceived for the grandest of organs, Laube performs his own organ version of Liszt's demanding B minor Piano Sonata. 'I first learnt it at the piano as a personal project,' he explains, 'never knowing it would see the concert stage – and at the organ! Every note of the original version is somehow represented in the organ transcription, just occasionally reorganised between the hands and feet. I spent hours at different organs experimenting with options until I found the right balance or the most idiomatic solution. But it's still a somewhat fluid process. I have some idea of what to expect at the Royal Albert Hall, but I'm certain the five- to nine-hour experience of deciding which stops to use for the sonata will be a deeply rewarding one between me, Liszt and "Father" Willis!'

Sunday 28 August

PROM 55 ☀
11.30am–c12.55pm • Royal Albert Hall

⬤ £8.50–£42 *(plus booking fee')*

THE ROYAL ALBERT HALL'S 'FATHER' WILLIS ORGAN

Wagner, transcr. W. J. Westbrook & Nathan Laube Tannhäuser – Grand March   *7'*

Franck Grande pièce symphonique   *25'*

Alkan 11 Grands préludes – No. 10: Scherzando   *5'*

Liszt, transcr. Nathan Laube Piano Sonata in B minor   *35'*

Nathan Laube *organ*

There will be no interval

Exciting young American organist Nathan Laube makes his Proms debut with a programme celebrating the expressive power of the Royal Albert Hall's mighty 'Father' Willis organ – the second-largest instrument of its kind in the UK. At the climax of the concert is Laube's own transcription of Liszt's brooding Sonata in B minor – perhaps the composer's greatest work for keyboard, its shape-shifting themes transformed with dazzling invention and variety. The concert also includes Franck's *Grande pièce symphonique* – an organ symphony dedicated to the great pianist and composer Charles-Valentin Alkan, whose own Scherzando from the *11 Grands préludes* is dedicated in return to Franck. The concert opens in a blaze with the Grand March from Wagner's opera *Tannhäuser* (see also Proms 31 and 72).

Sunday 28 August

PROM 56
7.30pm–c9.30pm • Royal Albert Hall

⬤ £9.50–£52 *(plus booking fee')*

ESKA

The South African Jazz Songbook

Artists to include:

Siyabonga Mthembu *vocals*
ESKA *vocals*
Theon Cross *tuba*

Metropole Orkest
Marcus Wyatt *conductor*

There will be one interval

Celebrated South African trumpeter, conductor and SAMA Award-winner Marcus Wyatt leads the Metropole Orkest in a showcase of the best of South African jazz – a cross-section of a vibrant and strikingly diverse scene. There will be music by artists including 'father of South African jazz' Hugh Masekela, Cry Freedom's Jonas Gwangwa, genre-crossing composer Abdullah Ibrahim, the Blue Notes' Dudu Pukwana and Johnny Dyani, and saxophonist Winston Mankunku. Vocalist Siyabonga Mthembu – lead singer of Shabaka and the Ancestors and performance art band The Brother Moves On – makes a special appearance, together with Mercury Prize-nominated singer ESKA and Sons of Kemet tuba player Theon Cross.

Monday 29 August

PROMS AT BIRMINGHAM ☀
1.00pm–c2.00pm • Bradshaw Hall

For ticket prices, see bbc.co.uk/promstickets

CLAIRE BARNETT-JONES

Horovitz Lady Macbeth – a scena *9'*
Smyth Lieder, Op. 4 *15'*
R. Clarke The Seal Man *6'*
Vaughan Williams Four Last Songs *9'*
Errollyn Wallen new work *c4'*
BBC co-commission: world premiere

Claire Barnett-Jones *mezzo-soprano*
Simon Lepper *piano*

There will be no interval

Finalist and winner of the Audience Prize at the 2021 BBC Cardiff Singer of the World competition, rising-star mezzo Claire Barnett-Jones has since gone on to major debuts at Glyndebourne, the Wigmore Hall and English National Opera, winning praise for her 'opulent tone'. She makes her Proms recital debut with pianist Simon Lepper in a concert of 20th- and 21st-century British song. The programme includes anniversary composer Vaughan Williams's *Four Last Songs*, their often mythology-inspired texts written by his wife Ursula, as well as Ethel Smyth's early Lieder, their expressive intimacy steeped in the German Romantic tradition the composer so admired.

Monday 29 August

PROM 57
7.30pm–c9.30pm • Royal Albert Hall

● **£14–£62** *(plus booking fee')*

MARY BEVAN

Bach Mass in B minor *108'*

Rachel Redmond *soprano*
Mary Bevan *soprano*
Iestyn Davies *counter-tenor*
Guy Cutting *tenor*
Matthew Brook *bass*

Choir of the Age of Enlightenment
Orchestra of the Age of Enlightenment
John Butt *conductor*

There will be no interval

Bach's Mass in B minor was the composer's last major work: the apotheosis of an entire career. Monumental in size and scope, a musical statement of faith that takes listeners from penitence and prayer to redemption and ecstatic rejoicing, it sits alongside Mozart's *Requiem*, Beethoven's *Missa solemnis* and Bach's own Passions as one of the greatest sacred works in the repertoire. Award-winning conductor John Butt, whose all-Bach Prom in 2019 was hailed as 'astonishing', directs the period-instrument Orchestra of the Age of Enlightenment and a team of leading soloists. *See 'Full Steam Ahead', pages 100–103.*

Spotlight on
John Butt • Prom 57

28 AUG — 29 AUG

'Bach's Mass in B minor is a bit like those half-baked loaves you take home and cook yourself, so that you can have them crusty or soft, however you want them. It has a slightly emergent quality, so that it's only finished in any successful performance.' John Butt, who conducts the work with the Orchestra of the Age of Enlightenment, means no disrespect to Bach. Instead, he's considering the questions surrounding the work that only a performance can answer. 'Also: what was it for? There are about four or five different theories now, and I don't think we'll ever truly know.'

As a musical scholar – he's Gardiner Professor of Music at the University of Glasgow, as well as Music Director of Edinburgh's Dunedin Consort and a global authority on German Baroque music – these are all questions that Butt considers deeply. As is the idea that Bach created the Mass in B minor – almost certainly his final piece – as the summation of his life's work. There's a lot of truth there, Butt believes. 'He always went out of his way to make his music good, of course, but there's a level of perfectionism here, a sense that he's reflecting not only on his different musical styles, but also on himself. It's a bit like a greatest hits, but the way they've been strung together and balanced against one another is so striking. If any piece of classical music can be considered universal, I think it's the Mass in B minor. It goes down so well across a wide range of cultures.'

Spotlight on
Timna Fibert
Proms 11, 23, 53, 60 & 68

As a trained audio describer, the first thing Timna Fibert often gets asked is: why do you need audio description at a concert? 'I usually answer: "Why are you going to a concert, when you could listen to a CD?" It's about giving people who are blind or partially sighted – or, in fact, anyone who finds it useful – a comparable concert experience to that of a sighted audience member – allowing them to participate in a shared, communal experience that they might otherwise feel excluded from.' Fibert is providing audio description for several Proms this season, including the Open Music Prom on 1 September. 'I'll describe how the musicians are seated, what they're wearing, the whole energy of the soloists and conductor. And, if anything unusual happens – say if somebody makes a grand entrance – I'll explain.' The question of whether or not to describe the music itself is tricky, she admits. 'What people want to hear varies with each person, but ultimately the audience is there for the music, so I keep description to an absolute minimum – I don't want to disturb that.'

How does she prepare for describing a concert? 'First of all, I make sure I have information on the performers and the music, and then I'll go to the final rehearsal and write my script based on what happens there. If something spontaneous happens at the concert itself, of course I'll endeavour to describe it, but generally I prefer not to have to improvise too much!'

Tuesday 30 August

PROM 58
8.00pm–c9.00pm • Royal Albert Hall

● £9.50–£52 *(plus booking fee')*

PUBLIC SERVICE BROADCASTING

Public Service Broadcasting
This New Noise   *c50'*
BBC commission: world premiere

Public Service Broadcasting

BBC Symphony Orchestra
Jules Buckley *conductor*

There will be no interval

A world premiere from cult London band Public Service Broadcasting. After the success of its 2019 Prom *The Race for Space*, the retro-futurist 'History Rock' group returns, joining Jules Buckley and the BBC Symphony Orchestra for *This New Noise* – a newly commissioned, album-length performance marking the centenary of the BBC. The band's signature combination of live acoustic and electronic elements with archival material creates soundscapes exploring key episodes in BBC Radio's past. Expect a multimedia spectacle in which rock concert meets history. *See 'Inform – Educate – Entertain', pages 56–58.*

🖥 *Broadcast on BBC Four on Friday 2 September*

20 Proms on BBC TV and available on BBC iPlayer

Wednesday 31 August

PROM 59
7.30pm–c9.25pm • Royal Albert Hall

● £14–£62 *(plus booking fee')*

JAMIE BARTON

Elgar The Dream of Gerontius   *100'*

Allan Clayton *tenor*
Jamie Barton *mezzo-soprano*
James Platt *bass*

Hallé Choir
London Philharmonic Choir
London Philharmonic Orchestra
Edward Gardner *conductor*

There will be no interval

Large-scale choral music is back this season, and it doesn't get bigger or more powerful than *The Dream of Gerontius*. Elgar's greatest choral work – the story of a dying man whose soul is guided by an angel towards heaven – is a powerful musical statement of faith and wonder. 'This is the best of me,' the composer wrote on his manuscript score, and the searing burst of realisation at Gerontius's eventual vision of God bears that out. The conductor is Edward Gardner, a distinguished interpreter of British music. *See 'Rolling with the Punches', pages 20–24.*

Thursday 1 September

PROM 60
7.30pm–c9.30pm • Royal Albert Hall

● £8.50–£42 (plus booking fee')

KWAMÉ RYAN

BBC Open Music Prom

Ruth Mariner creative director

BBC Concert Orchestra
Kwamé Ryan conductor

AD Audio-described by Timna Fibert
BSL British Sign Language-interpreted by Angie Newman

There will be one interval

Innovation, imagination and a reflection of today's audiences are at the heart of the first-ever BBC Open Music Prom. Tonight the reins are handed over to the 30 successful musicians and creatives (selected from over 1,300 applicants across the UK) who made it onto the BBC's new Open Music training and mentoring scheme. From a wealth of new ideas and outside-the-box thinking, the winning pitch is being developed with the support of creative director Ruth Mariner. The possibilities are many but what's certain is that nothing of this type will have been seen at the Proms before. See 'Open Score Policy', pages 60–63.

Every Prom live on BBC Radio 3 and available on BBC Sounds

Friday 2 September

PROM 61
7.30pm–c9.30pm • Royal Albert Hall

● £14–£62 (plus booking fee')

NICOLE CABELL

Walker Lilacs   15'

INTERVAL

Beethoven Symphony No. 9
in D minor, 'Choral'   70'

Nicole Cabell soprano
Raehann Bryce-Davis mezzo-soprano
Zwakele Tshabalala tenor
Ryan Speedo Green bass-baritone

Chineke! Voices
Chineke! Orchestra
Kevin John Edusei conductor

Praised for the 'special electricity' of its 2021 Proms performance, the Chineke! Orchestra – Europe's first majority-Black and ethnically diverse orchestra – returns to tackle one of the greats of the concert repertoire: Beethoven's Ninth Symphony. The orchestra is joined by newly formed sister ensemble Chineke! Voices – which makes its Proms debut – as well as soloists including Grammy-winning American bass-baritone Ryan Speedo Green and former BBC Cardiff Singer of the World winner Nicole Cabell. The concert opens with music by centenary composer George Walker – the first African American to win a Pulitzer Prize. Walker's Lilacs, which won him the award, is a setting of Walt Whitman and sees the composer at his most painterly and sensuous. See 'Rolling with the Punches', pages 20–24; 'A World of Music', pages 36–38.

🖥 Broadcast on BBC Four on Sunday 4 September

Spotlight on

Ryan Speedo Green • Prom 61

'With Beethoven's Ninth, I get to open the vocal part in the last movement.' Virginia-born bass-baritone Ryan Speedo Green is talking about Beethoven's famous 'Ode to Joy', which he performs with the Chineke! Orchestra on 2 September under Kevin John Edusei. 'It's kinda cool. Everyone knows that melody, and I get to be the one to give it to them first – it's a huge honour, but quite a pressure too!'

The Royal Albert Hall stage, however, is a long way from his underprivileged upbringing, including a stint in juvenile detention, as Green is aware. 'I feel like I'm a prime example of the American Dream. If it wasn't for opera, and for the teachers in my life who wanted me to get off the streets and see something other than pain and poverty, my life would be a completely different thing. Through opera I can put my passions, emotions and traumas into music.'

Green was a Principal Artist at the Vienna State Opera and has performed at New York's Metropolitan Opera. But he greatly enjoys performing in concert too. 'It's my chance to show my abilities 100 per cent as a singer without the distraction of costumes or sets.' There couldn't be a better piece than Beethoven's 'Choral' Symphony to convey his sense of positivity, he feels. 'It's about brotherhood and unity overcoming war and hatred. If we look back at mistakes we've made – whether it be racial injustice or homophobia or women's rights – we all have the opportunity to fix them.'

Saturday 3 September

**PROMS AND THE ENO AT
PRINTWORKS LONDON** ☀
3.00pm–c4.15pm & 8.00pm–c9.15pm

For ticket prices, see bbc.co.uk/promstickets

ANTHONY ROTH COSTANZO

Glass Handel

*An operatic spectacle juxtaposing works by
Philip Glass and Handel, featuring a specially
commissioned work by Philip Glass*

Programme to include excerpts from:

Philip Glass Songs from Liquid
Days; Monsters of Grace; The Fall of
the House of Usher; 1000 Airplanes
on the Roof

Handel Tolomeo; Flavio; Rinaldo;
Rodelinda; Amadigi

Anthony Roth Costanzo *counter-tenor*
George Condo *live painting*
Jason Singh *nature beatboxer/vocal sound
designer*
Justin Peck *choreographer*
Costumes by **Raf Simons**

The English National Opera Orchestra
Karen Kamensek *conductor*
James Bonas *stage director*

There will be no interval

*Created and co-produced with Anthony Roth Costanzo,
Cath Brittan, Visionaire and the English National Opera,
in collaboration with Printworks London*

Music, dance, theatre, video, audio soundscapes
and haute couture come together in a unique
project in the vast space of Printworks London.
Works by Handel and Philip Glass collide in a
spectacle conceived by Anthony Roth Costanzo
that includes a world premiere by Philip Glass.
See 'New Glass/Handel with Care', pages 18–19.

Saturday 3 September

PROM 62
7.00pm–c8.25pm • Royal Albert Hall

⚫ £18–£72 *(plus booking fee')*

KIRILL PETRENKO

Mahler Symphony No. 7   77'

Berliner Philharmoniker
Kirill Petrenko *conductor*

There will be no interval

One of the world's great orchestras, the
Berliner Philharmoniker, returns to the Proms
under Chief Conductor Kirill Petrenko with
Mahler's richly ambiguous Symphony No. 7.
Eeriness, eroticism, delirium and darkness
run through this mercurial work. At its centre
are two 'night music' movements – the first
black and heavy, the second lyrical and bright
with serenades – but there's also a musical
phantasmagoria of a Scherzo as well
as bucolic visions, love songs and a finale that
blazes with light and hope. 'The symphony must
be like the world,' Mahler once declared: 'it must
embrace everything.' And with his Seventh he
does. *See 'Full Steam Ahead', pages 100–103.*

Saturday 3 September

PROM 63 • LATE NIGHT 🌙
10.15pm–c11.30pm • Royal Albert Hall

⚫ £8.50–£26 *(plus booking fee')*

MARIUS NESET

Marius Neset
Geyser   *c65'*

BBC commission: world premiere

Marius Neset *saxophones*
Ivo Neame *piano*
Jim Hart *vibraphone/marimba/percussion*
Conor Chaplin *double bass*
Anton Eger *drums*

London Sinfonietta
Geoffrey Paterson *conductor*

There will be no interval

Drawing inspiration from artists as varied
as Frank Zappa, Pat Metheny, Mahler and
Messiaen, Norwegian virtuoso jazz saxophonist
Marius Neset has been credited with a
'voracious reinvention of jazz' and praised
for the 'breadth and depth of his emotional
shading'. Neset makes his Proms debut
alongside the rest of his quintet with the
world premiere of a major new work, *Geyser*.

**20 Proms on
BBC TV and
available on
BBC iPlayer**

Sunday 4 September

PROM 64 ☀

11.30am–c12.55pm • Royal Albert Hall

● **£14–£62** *(plus booking fee)*

SIR ANDRÁS SCHIFF

Beethoven

Piano Sonata No. 30
in E major, Op. 109   22'

Piano Sonata No. 31
in A flat major, Op. 110   22'

Piano Sonata No. 32
in C minor, Op. 111   27'

Sir András Schiff *piano*

There will be no interval

Continuing his sequence of Proms solo recitals, legendary pianist Sir András Schiff returns with Beethoven's final three sonatas. Written in 1820–22 alongside the *Missa solemnis (see Prom 69)* and the first sketches of the Ninth Symphony *(see Prom 61)*, this trilogy of late works represents the composer's last and most profound thoughts in a medium often seen as his most intimate and revealing: a 'vivid, detailed self-portrait', as Joseph Horowitz once described them. The lyrical, contained No. 30 contrasts with its more expansive successor – a hymn to hope in the face of despair – while No. 32 presents an Olympian conclusion to a monumental sequence of sonatas spanning a lifetime.

Sunday 4 September

PROM 65

7.30pm–c9.40pm • Royal Albert Hall

● **£18–£72** *(plus booking fee)*

KIRILL PETRENKO

Schnittke Viola Concerto   31'

INTERVAL

Shostakovich Symphony No. 10
in E minor   52'

Tabea Zimmermann *viola*

Berliner Philharmoniker
Kirill Petrenko *conductor*

In the second of two concerts, the Berliner Philharmoniker and Chief Conductor Kirill Petrenko perform two 20th-century Soviet masterpieces. Originally composed for Yuri Bashmet (whose name is woven through the work as a musical theme) and performed here by the great German violist Tabea Zimmermann, Schnittke's Viola Concerto brings out the elegiac quality of its solo instrument. The concerto's charged lament sets the scene for Shostakovich's 10th Symphony – a musical portrait of Stalin that convulses with horror, terror and brutality. But hope breaks through in the symphony's blazing close. *See 'Full Steam Ahead', pages 100–103.*

Every Prom live
on BBC Radio 3
and available on
BBC Sounds

Spotlight on

Tabea Zimmermann • Prom 65

It was way back in 1994 that German violist Tabea Zimmermann made her recording of Soviet composer Alfred Schnittke's intense, expressionistic Viola Concerto, which she brings to the BBC Proms on 4 September with the Berliner Philharmoniker and conductor Kirill Petrenko. 'Yes, I used to perform it very often. But I haven't now for a number of years. I'm very much looking forward to performing it with Kirill, though: his grasp of scores and the way he digs into detail is similar to my own approach.'

It's a hugely virtuosic piece that exerts an enormous emotional power on soloist and listeners alike. How does it feel returning to it after so long? 'I'm always changing my perspective on music,' Zimmermann says. 'Our life experiences change – the music we play, the books we read, the relationships we have. But I enjoy that. I hope I'm growing mentally all the time, and that gives me a different overview on any music I play. But, physically, things don't get easier with age!'

That's especially true of the Schnittke Concerto, whose frenzied, energetic central movement contrasts with intense introspection in its two outer movements. 'It requires a lot of stamina,' Zimmermann accepts, 'and you need to think carefully about how to use your body to maintain it. Schnittke wrote it for violist Yuri Bashmet, and he embedded the name "Bashmet" into the concerto's musical material. So, when I'm playing, I'm always thinking about my violist colleague too!'

Monday 5 September

📍 PROMS AT **GLASGOW** ☀
1.00pm–c2.00pm • Royal Conservatoire of Scotland, Stevenson Hall

For ticket prices, see bbc.co.uk/promstickets

TRIO GASPARD

Haydn Piano Trio in G minor, Hob. XV:19 *16'*

Smyth Piano Trio in D minor *28'*

Trio Gaspard

There will be no interval

In its Proms debut, the prize-winning young Trio Gaspard continues this year's Ethel Smyth focus with her Piano Trio in D minor. The influence of Smyth's studies in Leipzig and her encounters with Brahms, Dvořák and Clara Schumann are evident in this attractive early work, which owes much to the German Romantic tradition. A lyrical opening Allegro leads into a lullaby-like slow movement, a piquant, quicksilver scherzo and expansive finale. The concert opens with Haydn's Trio in G minor. Composed during the composer's 1795 visit to London, its intimate directness emerges most strikingly in its ruminative introduction and a radiant central andante.

Every Prom live on BBC Radio 3 and available on BBC Sounds

Monday 5 September

PROM 66
7.30pm–c9.30pm • Royal Albert Hall

⬤ £8.50–£42 *(plus booking fee')*

KARINA CANELLAKIS

Beethoven The Creatures of Prometheus – overture *6'*

Betsy Jolas bTunes for Nicolas *c15'*
BBC co-commission: world premiere

INTERVAL

Mahler Symphony No. 1 in D major *53'*

Nicolas Hodges *piano*

BBC Symphony Orchestra
Karina Canellakis *conductor*

'This is the sound of nature, not music,' Mahler wrote of the opening of his Symphony No. 1. Birds sing and flowers bloom, fruit ripens and a storm swells and dies away; nature's cycle from life to death runs through a work that fulfils the composer's all-encompassing vision of the symphony. Nature becomes a battleground in Beethoven's ballet *The Creatures of Prometheus*, as gods and mortals clash in the vivid landscape of Classical mythology. Karina Canellakis conducts the BBC Symphony Orchestra in a concert that also includes the world premiere of a new piano concerto by Franco-American composer Betsy Jolas: in the form of a suite evoking today's playlist-driven listening habits, these 'bTunes' are Betsy's answer to iTunes.

Tuesday 6 September

PROM 67
7.30pm–c9.50pm • Royal Albert Hall

⬤ £14–£62 *(plus booking fee')*

NICOLA BENEDETTI

Thomas Adès Three-Piece Suite from 'Powder Her Face' (Suite No. 1) *12'*

Wynton Marsalis Violin Concerto *43'*

INTERVAL

Britten Four Sea Interludes from 'Peter Grimes' *16'*

Bernstein Symphonic Dances from 'West Side Story' *24'*

Nicola Benedetti *violin*

Royal Scottish National Orchestra
Thomas Søndergård *conductor*

Rhythm – the strut of the tango, the explosive mambo, propulsive jigs and reels, even the swell of the sea – sets the pulse of this concert racing. Joining the Royal Scottish National Orchestra under Music Director Thomas Søndergård, and fresh from her Grammy-winning recording, Nicola Benedetti brings Wynton Marsalis's Violin Concerto to the Proms for the first time, with its electrifying fusion of the American bandleader's jazz influences and the Scottish folk music of the violinist's homeland. American jazz is also the starting point for the technicoloured brilliance of Bernstein's *West Side Story* and the sardonic First Suite from Thomas Adès's scandalous opera *Powder Her Face*. See 'Behold … The Sea!', pages 104–107.

🖵 *Broadcast on BBC Four on Friday 9 September*

Wednesday 7 September

PROM 68 ☀

11.00am–c12.00pm • Royal Albert Hall

● £8.50–£20 *(plus booking fee')*

THOMAS SØNDERGÅRD

Relaxed Prom

Nicola Benedetti *violin/presenter*

Royal Scottish National Orchestra
Thomas Søndergård *conductor*

There will be no interval

AD *Audio-described by Timna Fibert*
BSL *British Sign Language-interpreted by Angie Newman*
R *Relaxed performance*

Star violinist Nicola Benedetti returns with Thomas Søndergård and the Royal Scottish National Orchestra, this time as both soloist and presenter. This Relaxed Prom offers a chance to hear specially selected highlights of the music from last night's Prom *(see Prom 67)* – the explosive dances from Bernstein's *West Side Story*, Britten's evocative *Four Sea Interludes* and Wynton Marsalis's dance-infused Violin Concerto – in a more accommodating environment. See 'Behold … The Sea!', *pages 104–107.*

BBC Proms relaxed performances are designed to suit individuals or groups who feel more comfortable attending concerts in a relaxed environment. There is a relaxed attitude to noise and audience-members are free to leave and re-enter the auditorium at any point. There will be chill-out areas, where spaces are made for anyone needing a bit of quiet time before or during the performance. For full details, visit bbc.co.uk/proms.

Wednesday 7 September

PROM 69

7.00pm–c9.00pm • Royal Albert Hall

● £14–£62 *(plus booking fee')*

SIR JOHN ELIOT GARDINER

Beethoven Missa solemnis   81'

Lucy Crowe *soprano*
Ann Hallenberg *mezzo-soprano*
Giovanni Sala *tenor*
William Thomas *bass*

Monteverdi Choir
Orchestre Révolutionnaire et Romantique
Sir John Eliot Gardiner *conductor*

There will be no interval

Finding terror alongside spiritual awe, raising questions and doubts as well as proclaiming faith, Beethoven's *Missa solemnis* is a work of visceral power – a public statement of intensely private belief. 'From the heart – may it return to the heart!' the composer wrote at the top of a score that stretched the proportions and ambitions of the orchestral Mass to new limits. Sir John Eliot Gardiner – whose two benchmark recordings trace an ever-evolving relationship with the piece over many decades – conducts his period-instrument Orchestre Révolutionnaire et Romantique and the Monteverdi Choir.

🖵 **20 Proms on BBC TV and available on BBC iPlayer**

Spotlight on

Lucy Crowe • Prom 69

When Lucy Crowe steps onto the stage of the Royal Albert Hall on 7 September as soprano soloist in Beethoven's *Missa solemnis*, it won't be the first time she's performed the work there. 'The last time I sang it at the Proms I was pregnant with my son. To reach the high notes I had to hold my bump underneath to try and give myself some support. I actually went into labour four days later. I blame (or thank) Beethoven for the surprise birth of my son, five and a half weeks early. I think Ernie was rather disturbed by all the movement and noise!'

Indeed, it's a notoriously demanding piece for singers and orchestra alike. 'It was actually my first experience of singing Beethoven – and, boy, what a sing!' says Crowe. 'It's dramatic and powerful, yet gentle and mysterious – in your face, then subtle and spiritual. Vocally you need to channel your inner chameleon – the strength to sing loudly over the orchestra, but then float high, very quiet lines.'

Crowe regularly performs with her collaborators at this year's Proms, and has even recorded the *Missa solemnis* with them. 'I've been lucky enough to work with Sir John Eliot many times, and it's always challenging, rewarding and exhilarating. He expects our very best, so we all work to the highest level of technical ability, concentration and musicality. I also love working with the Orchestre Révolutionnaire et Romantique because my husband plays second horn in the orchestra!'

Spotlight on
Angel Blue • Prom 70

Los Angeles-born soprano Angel Blue makes her Proms debut as a performer on 8 September. But it's not her first time at the festival. 'I felt honoured to present the Proms on TV with Petroc Trelawny in 2015 – it was one of the most memorable times I have ever had attending live concerts. So this feels like coming full circle for me.'

And she's making her debut with a piece of music that has an equally personal resonance for her. 'I first got to know Barber's *Knoxville: Summer of 1915* when I was about 16. My dad bought me an album of Leontyne Price singing Barber, and I listened to it all the time: it was everything to me.' Blue went on to perform the piece at a local singing competition aged 19, coached by her mother and father, gospel singer and pastor Sylvester Blue. 'Little did I know that these memories would follow me for the rest of my life. My father passed away in 2006. What I particularly enjoy about performing *Knoxville* now is that my own memories of him and our close-knit family are brought back to life.'

Blue contrasts this with a piece that was entirely new to her: Valerie Coleman's *This Is Not a Small Voice*, which Blue premiered in Philadelphia earlier this year. 'It sets an epic poem by Sonia Sanchez, and Valerie's music is incredibly moving. She writes really well for the voice – I think, because she's a flautist, her ear is sensitive to vocal subtleties. The drama in her music also helps with telling the story of the poem.'

Thursday 8 September

PROM 70
7.30pm–c9.25pm • Royal Albert Hall

● £18–£72 *(plus booking fee')*

YANNICK NÉZET-SÉGUIN

Barber Knoxville: Summer of 1915 *16'*
Valerie Coleman This Is Not a Small Voice *10'*

INTERVAL

Beethoven Symphony No. 3 in E flat major, 'Eroica' *48'*

Angel Blue *soprano*

Philadelphia Orchestra
Yannick Nézet-Séguin *conductor*

Making its first Proms appearance for over a decade, the mighty Philadelphia Orchestra and Music Director Yannick Nézet-Séguin return with one of the greatest symphonies in the repertoire. With its 'strange modulations and violent transitions', Beethoven's 'Eroica' offers a passionate, protesting vision of heroism that surges with rebellious energy. Award-winning soprano Angel Blue is the soloist in an all-American first half that pairs Samuel Barber's 'lyric rhapsody' *Knoxville: Summer of 1915* – conjuring the sights, sounds and smells of the city as seen through the eyes of a small boy – with *This Is Not a Small Voice*, a setting by American composer Valerie Coleman of a poem by Philadelphia's former Poet Laureate Sonia Sanchez celebrating the power of Black voices, both individually and collectively. *See 'Full Steam Ahead', pages 100–103.*

Friday 9 September

PROM 71
7.30pm–c9.40pm • Royal Albert Hall

● £18–£72 *(plus booking fee')*

LISA BATIASHVILI

Rachmaninov The Isle of the Dead *20'*
Chausson Poème *16'*
Saint-Saëns Introduction and Rondo capriccioso *10'*

INTERVAL

Price Symphony No. 1 in E minor *38'*

Lisa Batiashvili *violin*

Philadelphia Orchestra
Yannick Nézet-Séguin *conductor*

Love, life and death collide in this second concert from the Philadelphia Orchestra and Music Director Yannick Nézet-Séguin. Lisa Batiashvili is the soloist in two of the great 19th-century violin concertos-in-miniature. Originally titled *The Song of Triumphant Love*, Chausson's *Poème* retains the rhapsodic spirit of its first sketches, while Saint-Saëns's *Introduction and Rondo capriccioso* is a Spanish-accented showcase of quicksilver brilliance and skill. By contrast, Rachmaninov's atmospheric *The Isle of the Dead* paints the scene of a ghostly ferryman transporting the souls of the departed to rest. Pioneering African American composer Florence Price's First Symphony – a work blending Classical forms with West African dances and spirituals – receives its Proms premiere in the second half. *See 'Full Steam Ahead', pages 100–103.*

Saturday 10 September

PROM 72

7.15pm–c10.15pm • Royal Albert Hall

○ **£30–105** *(plus booking fee*)*

LISE DAVIDSEN

SHEKU KANNEH-MASON

Last Night of the Proms 2022

Programme to include:

James B. Wilson 1922   c6'
BBC commission: world premiere

Coleridge-Taylor,
arr. Simon Parkin Deep River   5'

Wagner
Tannhäuser – 'Dich, teure Halle'   3'

Mascagni
Cavalleria rusticana – Easter Hymn   6'

Verdi
Macbeth – 'Vieni! t'affretta!'   6'

Carwithen
Overture 'ODTAA
(One Damn Thing After Another)'   9'

Davydov, arr. Simon Parkin
At the Fountain   4'

arr. Wood
Fantasia on British Sea-Songs   17'

Arne
Rule, Britannia!   4'

Elgar, arr. Anne Dudley
Pomp and Circumstance March No. 1
in D major ('Land of Hope
and Glory')   8'

Parry, orch. Elgar
Jerusalem   2'

arr. Britten
The National Anthem   3'

Trad.
Auld Lang Syne   2'

Lise Davidsen *soprano*
Sheku Kanneh-Mason *cello*

BBC Singers
BBC Symphony Chorus
BBC Symphony Orchestra
Dalia Stasevska *conductor*

There will be one interval

The world's biggest classical festival demands a big finale, and it doesn't get much bigger than the annual musical party that is the Last Night of the Proms. Expect fanfares and dances, anthems and arias, familiar classics and brand-new works from a concert that packs a whole season of highlights into just one event. Star cellist and former BBC Young Musician Sheku Kanneh-Mason and award-winning Norwegian soprano Lise Davidsen join the BBC Symphony Orchestra and Chorus and conductor Dalia Stasevska as soloists in a programme that includes arias by Wagner and Verdi and the radiant Easter Hymn from Mascagni's *Cavalleria rusticana*, as well as Doreen Carwithen's career-establishing 1945 concert overture *ODTAA* and the world premiere of a new work by fast-rising British composer James B. Wilson.

🖵 *First half on BBC Two, second half live on BBC One*

BBC
Last Night of the
Proms

Booking

Online
bbc.co.uk/promstickets
or royalalberthall.com

By phone
on 020 7070 4441 †

In person
at the Royal Albert
Hall Box Office

26 April
Create your
Proms Plan online

From 9.00am on Tuesday 26 April,
go to bbc.co.uk/promstickets and
fill in your Proms Planner. You must
complete your Plan by 11.59pm on
Friday 20 May in order to make a
booking. Creating a Plan does not
by itself result in a booking.

19 May
Book your
Promming Passes

From 9.00am on Thursday 19 May,
book your Season and Weekend
Promming (standing) Passes for the
Royal Albert Hall. (These passes are
not bookable in the Proms Planner.)

20 May
Book your CBeebies, Earth
and Relaxed Proms tickets

From 9.00am on Friday 20 May,
book your tickets for the:

- CBeebies Proms (Proms 11 & 12)
- Earth Proms (Proms 53 & 54)
- Relaxed Proms (Proms 23 & 68)

21 May
General Booking Opens

From 9.00am on Saturday 21 May,
submit your Proms Plan or book
online via bbc.co.uk/promstickets,
in person or by phone. See bbc.co.uk/
promstickets for details of how to book.

Tickets for 'Proms at' concerts will be
available directly from each venue, not
from the Royal Albert Hall. (These tickets
are not bookable via the Proms Planner.)

From this time you can also book your
free ticket for the 'Proms at Battersea'
BBC Young Composer concert (subject
to availability) via BBC Studio Audiences.
Visit bbc.co.uk/proms for details.

BOOKING FEES
Booking fees will be incurred on tickets purchased. At the time of going to print these fees are to
be confirmed. Please visit bbc.co.uk/promstickets from 26 April for full-booking fee details. They
will also be clearly displayed at the point of purchase on the Royal Albert Hall website.

† CALL COSTS
Standard geographic charges from landlines
and mobiles apply. All calls may be recorded and
monitored for training and quality-control purposes.

Royal Albert Hall ticket prices

Seated tickets for all BBC Proms concerts at the Royal Albert Hall fall into one of eight price bands, indicated beside each concert listing on pages 116–151. For Promming (standing) information, see opposite. See royalalberthall.com for further details.

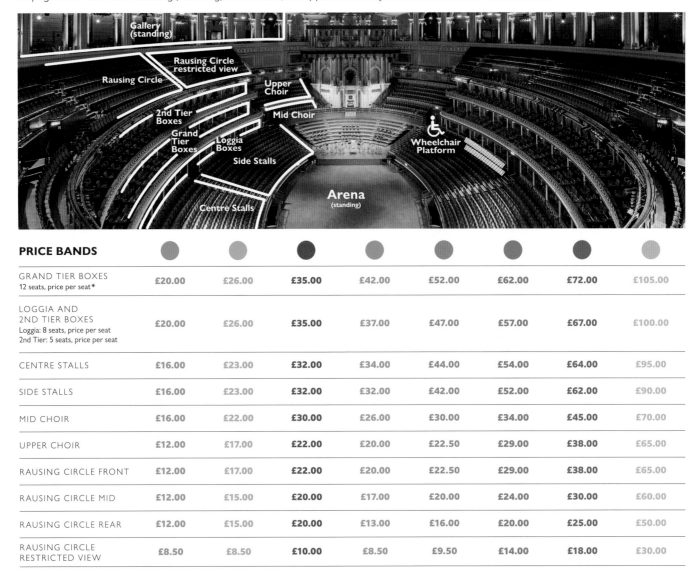

PRICE BANDS	●	●	●	●	●	●	●	●
GRAND TIER BOXES 12 seats, price per seat*	£20.00	£26.00	£35.00	£42.00	£52.00	£62.00	£72.00	£105.00
LOGGIA AND 2ND TIER BOXES Loggia: 8 seats, price per seat 2nd Tier: 5 seats, price per seat	£20.00	£26.00	£35.00	£37.00	£47.00	£57.00	£67.00	£100.00
CENTRE STALLS	£16.00	£23.00	£32.00	£34.00	£44.00	£54.00	£64.00	£95.00
SIDE STALLS	£16.00	£23.00	£32.00	£32.00	£42.00	£52.00	£62.00	£90.00
MID CHOIR	£16.00	£22.00	£30.00	£26.00	£30.00	£34.00	£45.00	£70.00
UPPER CHOIR	£12.00	£17.00	£22.00	£20.00	£22.50	£29.00	£38.00	£65.00
RAUSING CIRCLE FRONT	£12.00	£17.00	£22.00	£20.00	£22.50	£29.00	£38.00	£65.00
RAUSING CIRCLE MID	£12.00	£15.00	£20.00	£17.00	£20.00	£24.00	£30.00	£60.00
RAUSING CIRCLE REAR	£12.00	£15.00	£20.00	£13.00	£16.00	£20.00	£25.00	£50.00
RAUSING CIRCLE RESTRICTED VIEW	£8.50	£8.50	£10.00	£8.50	£9.50	£14.00	£18.00	£30.00

Booking fees will be incurred on tickets purchased. At the time of going to print these fees are to be confirmed. Please visit bbc.co.uk/promstickets from 26 April for full booking-fee details. They will also be clearly displayed at the point of purchase on the Royal Albert Hall website.
*As most Grand Tier Boxes are privately owned, availability is limited.

Advance seats

There is a Prom for every music-lover, whether you're a first-timer or a seasoned regular. To view the whole season at a glance, see the inside front cover. Advance seats start from just £8.50 (plus booking fee).

Stand on the day

The popular tradition of Promming (standing in the Arena or Gallery areas of the Royal Albert Hall) is central to the unique and informal atmosphere of the BBC Proms. Around 1,000 standing places in the Arena and Gallery are available on the day of each concert, for just £6.00 (plus booking fee). You can book up to two tickets online on the day of the concert. Visit bbc.co.uk/proms for more details.

Save money by buying a Season or Weekend Promming Pass (not all Proms are included). Please see new terms and conditions by visiting bbc.co.uk/proms.

Promming tickets for 'Proms at' venues are available. Visit bbc.co.uk/promstickets for details.

Online booking

The 'Select Your Own Seat' option is not available via the Proms Planner or during the first few days that Proms tickets are on sale. You will be allocated the best available places within your chosen seating area.

It is not possible to book entire boxes online. If you would like to book a complete box, call the Box Office on 020 7070 4441.

18s and under go half-price

Tickets for persons aged 18 and under can be purchased at half-price in any seating area of the Royal Albert Hall except the Last Night. (Not applicable to Promming tickets.)

Great savings for groups

Groups of 10 or more attending Royal Albert Hall concerts can claim a 5% discount on the price of selected tickets (not including the Last Night). Call the Group Booking Information Line on 020 7070 4408 for details.

'Proms at' concerts

Tickets for 'Proms at' concerts will be available directly from each venue at 9.00am on Saturday 21 May. Prices will vary for each venue. See bbc.co.uk/promstickets for details.

Last Night of the Proms

Owing to high demand, the majority of seated tickets for the Last Night of the Proms are allocated by ballot, as follows:

The Five-Concert Ballot

Customers who purchase tickets for at least five other concerts at the Royal Albert Hall are eligible to enter the Five-Concert Ballot. For details on how to enter, see bbc.co.uk/promstickets. The Five-Concert Ballot closes at midnight on Thursday 9 June.

If you require a wheelchair space for the Last Night, you will still need to book for five other concerts, but you must phone the Access Information Line (020 7070 4410) before 9.00pm on Thursday 9 June to enter the separate ballot for wheelchair spaces.

The Open Ballot

One hundred Centre Stalls seats (priced £95.00 each, plus booking fee) and 100 Front Circle seats (priced £65.00 each, plus booking fee) for the Last Night of the Proms at the Royal Albert Hall will be allocated by Open Ballot, which closes at midnight on Thursday 7 July.

Please complete the official Open Ballot Form, which is available to download from bbc.co.uk/promstickets.

General availability for the Last Night

Any remaining tickets for the Last Night will go on sale at 9.00am on Friday 15 July by phone or online only. Only one application (for a maximum of two tickets) can be made per household. There is exceptionally high demand for Last Night tickets, but returns occasionally become available.

Promming (standing) at the Last Night

Whole Season Promming Passes include admission to the Last Night. A limited allocation of Last Night standing tickets (priced £6.00, plus booking fee) are also reserved for Prommers who have attended five or more concerts (in the Arena or the Gallery). They are eligible to purchase one ticket each for the Last Night on presentation of their used tickets (which will be retained) at the Box Office. For details, see bbc.co.uk/promstickets.

On the night

A limited number of Promming tickets will be available on the Last Night itself (priced £6.00, one per person). No previous ticket purchases are necessary.

Promming is easy!

Tickets not available for your favourite Prom? Don't give up: get Promming (standing) tickets on the day for £6.00 (plus booking fee). Around 1,000 tickets will be released online on the day of the concert (maximum two per person).

How to Prom

Visit bbc.co.uk/promstickets for our guide to Promming, and information on places for wheelchair-users and ambulant disabled concert-goers.

Visit bbc.co.uk/ promstickets for full details of how to book, booking fees and terms and conditions

If you have any questions regarding accessibility at the Proms, call the Access Information Line on 020 7070 4410

Access at the Proms

ACCESS INFORMATION LINE
020 7070 4410 (9.00am–9.00pm daily).

Full information on the facilities offered to disabled concert-goers at the Royal Albert Hall is available online at royalalberthall.com or by calling the Access Information Line. The Royal Albert Hall has a Silver award from the Attitude is Everything Charter of Best Practice.

All disabled concert-goers (and one companion) receive a 50% discount on all ticket prices for all Proms concerts (except for Arena and Gallery areas at the Royal Albert Hall). To book, call the Access Information Line or purchase in person at the Royal Albert Hall.

Throughout the Proms season at the Royal Albert Hall 12 spaces will be available to book for wheelchair-users and companions on a designated wheelchair platform situated in front of Loggias Boxes 31–33. Depending on the Prom, between 18 and 25 additional wheelchair spaces will be available in the Stalls and the Circle. To book, call the Access Information Line or visit the Royal Albert Hall Box Office in person.

For information on wheelchair spaces available for the Last Night of the Proms via the Five-Concert Ballot, see page 155.

The Gallery can accommodate up to four wheelchair-users.

A limited number of car parking spaces close to the Hall can be reserved by disabled concert-goers; contact the Access Information Line to book.

Ramped venue access is available at Doors 1, 3, 8, 9 and 12. The most convenient set-down point for vehicle arrival is near Door 3.

Public lifts are located at Doors 1 and 8. All bars and restaurants are wheelchair-accessible.

The Royal Albert Hall auditorium has an infra-red system with a number of personal headsets available for use with or without hearing aids. These are also available for Proms 11, 23, 53, 60 and 68, which will be audio-described. Headsets can be collected on arrival from the Information Desk on the Ground Floor at Door 6.

Assistance dogs are very welcome and can be easily accommodated in the boxes. If you prefer to sit elsewhere, call the Access Information Line for advice. The Royal Albert Hall stewards will be happy to look after your dog while you enjoy the concert.

Transfer wheelchairs are available for customer use. The Royal Albert Hall has busy corridors and therefore visitors using mobility scooters are asked to enter via Door 3 or Door 8 and will be offered a transfer wheelchair on arrival. Scooters can be stored in designated places. We are unable to offer charging facilities for scooters.

To request any of the above services, call the Access Information Line or complete an accessibility request form online at royalalberthall.com 48 hours before you attend. Alternatively you can make a request upon arrival at the Information Desk at Door 6, subject to availability.

BSL Assisted Proms

Six Proms will be British Sign Language-interpreted (see opposite). Book tickets for these Proms online in the usual way. If you require good visibility of the signer, choose the Stalls Signer Area when selecting tickets, or request by calling the Access Information Line.

For information about the Relaxed concerts, including Audio Description services, visit bbc.co.uk/proms.

Accessibility at the Proms

BSL **British Sign Language-interpreted Proms**	Proms 11 & 12 (CBeebies Proms) • 23 July Prom 23 • 3 August Prom 53 (Earth Prom) • 27 August Prom 60 (BBC Open Music Prom) • 1 September Prom 68 • 7 August
AD **Audio-described Proms**	Prom 11 (CBeebies Prom) • 23 July Prom 23 • 3 August Prom 53 (Earth Prom) • 27 August Prom 60 (BBC Open Music Prom) • 1 September Prom 68 • 7 August
S **Surtitled Proms**	Prom 13 (The Wreckers) • 24 July Prom 19 (Il tabarro) • 30 July
R **Relaxed performances**	Proms 11 & 12 (CBeebies Proms) • 23 July Prom 23 (Aurora Orchestra) • 3 August Prom 68 (RSNO) • 7 September

For further information, please visit bbc.co.uk/proms. If you would like to discuss additional access requirements, call the Access Information Line (020 7070 4410).

BBC Proms Festival Guide – Braille and large-print formats

Braille versions of this Festival Guide are available in two parts, 'Articles' and 'Concert Listings/Booking Information', priced £4.49 and £4.50 respectively. For more information and to order, call the RNIB Helpline on 0303 123 9999.

A text-only large-print version of this Festival Guide is available, priced £8.99. To order, call Deborah Fether on 07716 225658, or email PromsPublications@bbc.co.uk. (Allow 10 working days for delivery.)

The Guide is also available to purchase as an eBook and in ePDF format. Both are compatible with screen readers and text-to-speech software. Visit bloomsbury.com/uk for details.

BBC Proms concert programmes in large print

Large-print concert programmes can be purchased on the night (at the same price as standard programmes), if ordered at least five working days in advance.

Large-print sung texts and librettos (where applicable) are available with the purchase of a standard programme, if ordered at least five working days in advance. This excludes surtitled Proms, for which librettos are not printed.

To order, call Deborah Fether on 07716 225658, or email PromsPublications@bbc.co.uk. Programmes and texts will be left for collection at the Door 6 Merchandise Desk one hour before the concert begins.

A Royal Albert Hall steward will be happy to read the concert programme to visually impaired visitors. Call the Access Information Line (020 7070 4410) or complete an accessibility request form online at royalalberthall.com 48 hours before you attend.

Royal Albert Hall

Kensington Gore, London SW7 2AP
www.royalalberthall.com • 020 7070 4441

The Royal Albert Hall of Arts and Sciences was officially opened by Queen Victoria on 29 March 1871. When, in 1867, Victoria laid the foundation stone for the building, she announced that it was to be named after her husband, Prince Albert, who had died six years earlier.

The Hall has hosted 25 suffragette meetings, and many of the world's leading figures in music, dance, sport and politics have appeared on its stage. These include Winston Churchill, the Dalai Lama, Emmeline Pankhurst and Nelson Mandela, as well as various royals and world leaders.

The BBC Proms has called the Royal Albert Hall its home since 1941, after the Queen's Hall was gutted by fire in an air-raid. The Hall has since hosted over 4,500 Proms concerts.

Latecomers
Latecomers will only be admitted if and when there is a suitable break in the performance.

Security
Please do not bring large bags to the Royal Albert Hall. All bags and visitors may be subject to security checks as a condition of entry.

Children under 5
Everyone is welcome at the CBeebies Proms (Proms 11 and 12) and Relaxed Proms (Proms 23 and 68). Out of consideration for audience and artists, we recommend that children attending other Proms are aged 5 and over.

Dress code
Come as you are: there is no dress code at the Proms.

Proms merchandise and programmes
Merchandise is available at Doors 6 and 12 and on the Rausing Circle level at Doors 4 and 8. Programmes are on sale throughout the building. Merchandise and programmes are also available online at shop.royalalberthall.com.

South Kensington (Piccadilly, Circle & District Lines); Gloucester Road (Piccadilly, Circle & District Lines); High Street Kensington (Circle & District Lines)

Enjoy a wide range of food and drink from two and a half hours before each concert – see royalalberthall.com

Cloakroom available. A charge of £1.00 per item applies. Cloakroom season tickets, priced £20.40, are also available (conditions apply – see royalalberthall.com)

Wheelchair-accessible (see page 156 for details)

Battersea Arts Centre • 30 July & 8 August

Lavender Hill, London SW11 5TN
www.bac.org.uk • 020 7223 2223

⊖ Clapham Junction (Overground; National Rail);
Clapham Common (Northern Line);
Stockwell (Victoria Line)

🥤 Bars on site; food and drink available

👔 Cloakroom available

♿ Wheelchair-accessible

Hall for Cornwall • 25 July

Back Quay, Truro TR1 2LL
www.hallforcornwall.co.uk • 01872 262466

🚆 Truro (National Rail)

🥤 Bar on site

👔 Cloakroom available

♿ Wheelchair-accessible

Printworks London • 3 September

Surrey Quays Road, London SE16 7PJ
www.printworkslondon.co.uk • 020 8498 4934

⊖ Canada Water (Overground; Jubilee Line);
Surrey Quays (Overground)

🥤 Bars and food stalls on site

👔 Locker/cloakroom facilities
available on site

♿ Wheelchair-accessible

Bradshaw Hall, Royal Birmingham Conservatoire • 29 August

200 Jennens Road, Birmingham B4 7XR
www.bcu.ac.uk/conservatoire • 0121 331 5901

≋ Birmingham Moor Street (National Rail)

📱 Bar on site

👔 Cloakroom available

♿ Wheelchair-accessible

Stevenson Hall, Royal Conservatoire of Scotland • 5 September

100 Renfrew Street, Glasgow G2 3DB
www.rcs.ac.uk • 0141 332 4101

≋ Glasgow Queen Street (National Rail);
Glasgow Central (National Rail)

📱 Café-bar on site

👔 Cloakroom available

♿ Wheelchair-accessible

Royal Welsh College of Music & Drama • 15 August

Castle Grounds, Cathays Park, Cardiff CF10 3ER
www.rwcmd.ac.uk • 029 2034 2854

≋ Cathays (National Rail);
Cardiff Queen Street (National Rail);
Cardiff (National Rail)

📱 Bar on site

♿ Wheelchair-accessible

Sage Gateshead • 23 July

St Mary's Square, Gateshead NE8 2JR
www.sagegateshead.com • 0191 443 4666

≉ Newcastle Central (National Rail; Metro);
Manors (National Rail; Metro); Gateshead (Metro)

🍸 Bar on site

👔 Cloakroom available

♿ Wheelchair-accessible

St George's Bristol • 1 August

Great George Street, Bristol BS1 5RR
www.stgeorgesbristol.co.uk • 0117 929 4929

≉ Bristol Temple Meads (National Rail);
Clifton Down (National Rail)

🍸 Bar on site; food and drink available

♿ Wheelchair-accessible

St George's Hall, Liverpool • 22 August

St George's Place, Liverpool L1 1JJ
www.stgeorgeshallliverpool.co.uk
events.stgeorgeshall@liverpool.gov.uk

≉ Liverpool Lime Street (National Rail; City Line);
Liverpool Central (National Rail; Northern & Wirral lines)

🍸 Bar on site

👔 Cloakroom available

♿ Wheelchair-accessible (except Balcony)

Waterfront Studio, Belfast • 18 July

2 Lanyon Place, Belfast BT1 3WH
www.waterfront.co.uk

🚉 Lanyon Place (NI Railways)

🍸 Bar on site

♿ Wheelchair-accessible

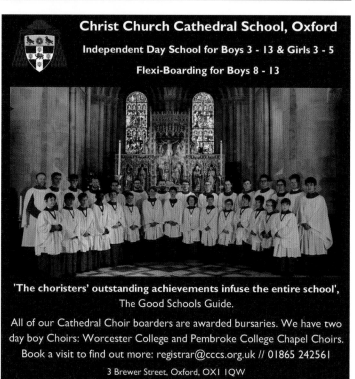

A CLUB
WITHOUT
COMPARISON

The Royal Over-Seas League is a unique, not-for-profit private membership organisation.

We celebrate international friendship through social, music and art programmes including the prestigious ROSL Annual Music Competition. Members enjoy first class performances from international young musicians, talks and visual art exhibitions; all within the surroundings of a Grade-I historic clubhouse and garden, located in the heart of St James's, London.

Preferential rates – Quote 'FESTIVAL 2022'

Over-Seas House
Park Place
St James's Street
London SW1A 1LR

www.rosl.org.uk   020 7408 0214
rosl1910   royaloverseaslondon

Soprano Milly Forrest, winner of the Singers Prize in the 2021 ROSL Annual Music Competition

ROSL
ROYAL OVER-SEAS LEAGUE
ESTD 1910

Parkhouse Award presents

TRIO BOHÉMO

· **Thursday 29 September 2022**
7.30pm, Stoller Hall, Manchester
Piano trios by: **Piazzolla, Martinů & Rachmaninov**
stollerhall.com/whats-on/trio-bohemo/

Wednesday 26 October 2022
1pm, Wigmore Hall, London
Piano trios by: **Shostakovich, Smetana & Schoenfield**
Wigmore-hall.org.uk

BBC

TEN PIECES

GET CREATIVE WITH
CLASSICAL MUSIC

Start your classical music adventure at
bbc.co.uk/tenpieces

BBC Ten Pieces opens up the world of
classical music for **7- to 14-year-olds**

Photograph: Pete Dabbs

Index of Artists

Index of
Artists

Index of Artists

Index of Works

Index of Works

BBC Proms 2022

Director, BBC Proms David Pickard
Controller, BBC Radio 3 Alan Davey
Personal Assistant Yvette Pusey

Editor, BBC Radio 3 Emma Bloxham

Head of Marketing, Learning and Publications Kate Finch

Business Sanoma Evans (Business Advisor), Tricia Twigg (Co-ordinator)

Concerts and Planning Helen Heslop (Manager), Hannah Donat (Artistic Producer), Alys Jones, Helen White (Event Producers), Victoria Gunn (Event Co-ordinator)

Marketing Emily Caket (Manager), Chloe Jaynes (Executive)

Press and Communications Camilla Dervan (Communications Manager), Samantha Johnston (Publicist), Juliet Martin (Assistant Publicist)

Learning Lauren Creed, Ellara Wakely (Senior Learning Managers), Alison Dancer, Melanie Fryer, Laura Mitchell (Learning Managers), Siân Bateman, Catherine Humphrey (Learning Co-ordinators), Chifaa Khelfaoui, Martin O-Whyte (Learning and Community Engagement Trainees)

Music Television Suzy Klein (Head of Commissioning, BBC Music TV), Livewire Pictures Ltd (Production)

Digital Rory Connolly (Commissioning Executive, BBC Pop), Rhian Roberts (Head of Content Commissioning, Speech and Classical Music), David Prudames (Assistant Commissioner, BBC Music Digital)

BBC Music Library Tim Auvache, Anne Butcher, Raymond Howden, Alison John, Michael Jones, Richard Malton, Claire Martin, Steven Nunes, Alex Pavelich, David Russell, Joseph Schultz

Commercial Rights & Business Affairs Simon Brown, Sue Dickson, Hilary Dodds, Ashley Smith, Pamela Wise

BBC Proms Publications
Publishing Manager Christine Webb
Editorial Manager Edward Bhesania
Sub-Editor Timmy Fisher
Publications Designer Reenie Basova
Publications Co-ordinator Deborah Fether

Advertising Cabbells (020 3603 7930); cabbells.co.uk
Cover illustration Mother Design/BBC/Amber Vittoria
Published by BBC Proms Publications, Room 3015, Broadcasting House, London W1A 1AA
Distributed by Bloomsbury Publishing, 50 Bedford Square, London WC1B 3DP

Printed by APS Group

APS Group holds ISO 14001 environmental management, FSC® and PEFC certifications. Printed using vegetable-based inks on FSC-certified paper. Formed in 1993 as a response to concerns over global deforestation, FSC (Forest Stewardship Council®) is an independent, non-governmental, not-for-profit organisation established to promote the responsible management of the world's forests. For more information, please visit www.fsc-uk.org.

In line with the BBC's sustainability strategy, the BBC Proms is actively working with partners and suppliers towards being a more sustainable festival.

ISBN 978-1-912114-11-5   © BBC 2022. All details correct at time of going to press.